SOCIAL
RESPONSIBILITY
&
INVESTMENTS

SOCIAL RESPONSIBILITY & INVESTMENTS

Charles W. Powers

nashville   Abingdon Press   new york

SOCIAL RESPONSIBILITY AND INVESTMENTS

Copyright © 1971 by Abingdon Press

ISBN 0-687-38925-9

Library of Congress Catalog Card Number: 72-148859

SET UP, PRINTED, AND BOUND BY THE
PARTHENON PRESS, AT NASHVILLE,
TENNESSEE, UNITED STATES OF AMERICA

PREFACE

"Why not a book on the investment responsibilities of all nonprofit institutions?" asked one early reader of the outline of this book. Since this is a book addressed first of all and unabashedly to churchmen, the question deserves an answer. It is true that the dearth of written material on the issue of social investment policy may mean that this book will serve, by default, as the introduction of the issue to persons concerned about social investment policies of many nonchurch institutions. The material covered in chapters 1, 3, 4, and 5 and Appendix A is as relevant to the foundation, the university and, perhaps, the pension board, as it is to the church. Still, even in these sections there are specific allusions to the special responsibilities and problems of the church.

It has become increasingly clear to me as I work with the problems attendant to the development of social investment policies for universities and watch closely the exciting stirrings in the nation's foundations that the various types of nonprofit institutions have their own problems and advantages in the field. In the winter of 1969 I coauthored an article, "Institutions, Investments, and Integrity," [1] which minimized these differences and exhorted all such institutions to evolve a social investment approach; the implicit assumption there was that, on this question, nonprofit institutions could develop a common policy. While that article served its purpose in raising the issue, this book is, hopefully, a more careful and discriminating analysis which takes as seriously the differences among these types of institutions as the earlier article took the similarities.

Even with this restricted focus, this is still a book of "elements." No reader should expect to find here a definitive policy for the social investment funds of his local church, his denomination, seminary, church pension board —or for his own funds. It should be noted here a few of the many reasons why this is so.

1. Many issues are simply not dealt with here—and yet some of them are the "first-level" issues for any churchman. For example, should a church (or a church-

[1] Jon P. Gunnemann, *The Christian Century*, January 29, 1969.

man) hold investments at all? Which biblical passage one turns to for an answer will depend on his whole religious orientation. Should the Christian take literally Christ's advice to the rich young man and give all he has to the poor? (Matt. 19:21) Should the Christian take literally his admonition "Do not lay up for yourselves treasures on earth, where moth and rust consume"? (Matt. 6:19-21) Or does such a view abdicate the stewardship responsibilities indicated in the parable of the talents, where the Master praises the investing servant? (Matt. 25:14-30) Presumably Christians agree that they are answerable to the Psalmist's exhortation to "defend the poor and fatherless; do justice to the afflicted and needy" (Ps. 82:3 KJV), but how investments function in this effort is disputed. In one sense, these questions are irrelevant, for the church is (or has allowed itself to be) legally locked into its role as an investor (see chapter 5); but a church's view of wealth, informed by a variety of biblical understandings, will affect what it now does with those funds. This book avers that since churches will continue to hold investments, it is essential that the investing function be Christianly responsible—or at least as responsible as external constraints permit.

2. Another reason why this book can offer only "elements" is that it explores a very new field. The "state of the art" is primitive. Information about the relatively few initiatives by American institutions to incorporate the notion of "social responsibility" into investment policy is difficult to obtain and interpret. Although the author has

made a strenuous effort to gather such information, this is not a complete report on the subject. One who has been involved in a new and growing social movement often has a difficult choice. He can wait until all the evidence is in and until he has covered every possible angle before putting pen to paper, or at an early date he can make urgently needed clarification and information available to a wide public in the hope that his work can be a part of the developments, not merely a history of them. The second course is, I believe, the obligation of a social ethicist.

3. Furthermore, the notion of social investment involves a whole range of specialized fields of knowledge. Among them are law (trust, corporation, administrative), history, economics, business, sociology, political science, ethics, and—for church investment policy—theology. While I have had the extraordinary opportunity of working with highly qualified persons from all of these fields, I cannot claim the interdisciplinary expertise required for a definitive treatment of the subject. Hence, again—"elements."

On the other hand, this is not a book of random fragments. The elements are ordered to lead in a specific direction. The Introduction briefly sketches social investment initiatives already made by the churches. The first section offers a theoretical framework for the whole social investment notion. The first chapter in this section is a brief historical interpretation of the American economic and political developments which have created the setting in which the contemporary investor finds himself.

The second chapter looks at the church as one part of the community of private nonprofit institutions which invest, and then suggests that the various churches should define their investment responsibilities in terms of their own theological and ethical understandings. This chapter serves primarily to open the door for more substantive theological and ethical work.

The next two sections have a more specific and technical character—they get down to cases. The second section describes the various options open to a church seeking to use its prerogatives as an investor for social ends. The list here is not exhaustive, but does provide a framework for further work. The third section explores institutional and legal impediments which may deter the churches as they pursue the options described in the previous section, and outlines some ways of overcoming these impediments. It also examines briefly a variety of organizational mechanisms for structuring social investment policies and implementation. Finally, it notes the lack of adequate information in the field, suggests some ways of rectifying this situation, and then turns to the special problems and opportunities of the *individual* investor seeking to make his own practices responsible.

Appendix A presents a brief schematic outline of corporate responsibility to help the reader think through his own views on what the corporation should be doing to further social ends. Appendix B is a short collection of some of the important documents emanating from the churches in the social investment field.

Precisely because there is so little written on this subject, I have been heavily dependent upon many people with or against whom I have honed my ideas in a wide variety of contexts. I can only mention a few of them here: John C. Bennett, Charles Bonos, Kingman Brewster, Jr., Charles Dryden, Clifton Graves, Jon P. Gunnemann, James M. Gustafson, David W. Hornbeck, R. Paul Ramsey, John G. Simon, Samuel Slie, Alice Tepper, James Tobin, William Treiber, and Frank White. I have learned very different kinds of things from these people, but am grateful to all of them.

In addition, I appreciate the help given me by my colleagues, William Horvath and Jean Rittmueller. They worked tirelessly through a hot New Haven summer to straighten out my thoughts and straighten up my prose. I also want to thank Mrs. Judith McBride who transcribed many of these words from handwriting to typescript.

On a more personal note, my family's—and especially my late father's—abiding concern for the plight of persons whom our society tends to forget or ignore helped foster in me the moral and religious sense which I hope this book reflects. Finally, most important to the writing of this book and everything else are Libby and Laura.

CHARLES W. POWERS
New Haven, 1971

CONTENTS

INTRODUCTION: A BRIEF SURVEY OF SOCIAL INVESTMENT INITIATIVES IN THE CHURCHES[1]

Where did the movement toward a socially aware use of church investment funds begin? Where does it now stand? Since social investment initiatives are just now "surfacing," it is extraordinarily difficult to answer these questions. Enough information is available, however, to provide some indication of where the churches have been and what they are doing now. Surely, there is enough to

[1] The preparation of this section has been aided by the responses to a letter sent by the author to the heads of 28 denominations. Replies were received from 20 denominations. The survey of the denominations shows that churches are caught in a quagmire of legal, economic, and moral issues which have paralyzed many of them even before they have begun.

document the statement that a trend to examine the social and moral implications of church investment policies is growing. Enough information is also available to suggest that the skills which will be necessary to the task are just now being mobilized.

Since the late 1800's, some churches have simply refrained from investment relationships with companies producing liquor and tobacco. One finds such a policy, explicitly spelled out or implicitly applied, in many churches today, including the Reorganized Church of Jesus Christ of the Latter Day Saints, the Methodist Missions Board, the Church of the Brethren, a number of boards of the United Presbyterian Church, U.S.A., the First Church of Christ, Scientist, the Church of the Nazarene, the Mennonite Foundation and, most recently (1963), the National Council of Churches. For many of these churches (the Methodists, Mennonites, and Christian Scientists) this earliest "social investment policy" was directly related to the theological teachings of the church.

In the early 1930's a number of churches raised the question of the social consequences of investment policies. At that time decisions were made *not* to build upon the existing precedents, but to seek a high return for the church in the belief that the money made available to church program endeavors would be a more effective approach to the issues under discussion (one of which was the role of munitions manufacturers in public policy-formation—an issue analogous to the contemporary concern about defense contracts).

Introduction

The issue remained dormant until the early 1960's when the National Committee on Tithing in Investments (NCTI), with an illustrious membership that included many leading churchmen, raised the issue in clear and convincing terms by proposing that churches, along with other charitable institutions and individuals, invest ten percent of their investment assets in open housing projects. Purchase orders for shares of MREIT, the first large-scale, private, nonprofit initiative in integrated housing, have slowly trickled in. The NCTI initiative made more headlines than headway, however.

The churches first really confronted the issue in its contemporary garb when, in the spring of 1966, two students from Union Theological Seminary persuaded hundreds of students in all Morningside Heights educational institutions to petition New York banks not to renew their revolving credit arrangement with the South African government. A large number of church investment boards met with the students during this period, and the bank campaign began to both flower and bear fruit. A. Philip Randolph headed a committee of many celebrities and churchmen which carried on the initiative, and a number of church institutions (the Methodist Board of Missions was the first major one) severed a variety of banking relationships with banks involved in the consortium.[2] However one views the effectiveness of this effort, the question

[2] See chapter 3 for further discussion of this campaign. A description of its initial stages is included in an article by David W. Hornbeck and the author, "Another Perspective on Seminary Social Action," *Theological Education,* February, 1968.

of social investment policy now lay unambiguously before a number of church investment boards.

The next important development occurred in the spring of 1967 when the "church-as-concerned-stockholder" mode surfaced. Here the United Church of Christ, the Unitarian-Universalists, and the Methodists took the lead in questioning Eastman-Kodak's handling of its agreement with FIGHT (Freedom, Integration, God, Honor—Today) in Rochester (see discussion, chapter 3). The churches' concern and the publicity it generated seem to have made an important difference. Earlier, in March of 1967, the Unitarians had appointed the first potentially effective social investment committee (the Committee on Investment Policy and Social Responsibility). This group seemed destined to set the pace for the churches, until it ran into the "prudent man" barrier, which it struggled to circumvent for three years before dissolving itself (see discussion, chapter 5). Nevertheless social investment efforts of all sorts were beginning to move with alacrity. Resolutions in the 1967 General Synod of the United Church of Christ pointed out a number of areas where that church could link its economic management to its social concern.

But in this period the major thrust seems to have been coming, not from top down, but from the grass roots up. Church bodies in many localities began to deposit some of their funds in black banks, and many became nonprofit sponsors of low- and middle-income housing construction and rehabilitation. Indeed, individual members, local congregations, and regional bodies provided much of the pressure for national denomination action on the South African issue as it developed over a three-year period. These local expressions have generally included not only approval, but much disapproval of social investment initiatives.

As one denominational executive put it: "I do not know of any *ad hoc* moves among the churches in our denomination seeking more socially responsible investment policy, but I would not doubt that there are some. The criticism we get is on the other side, namely, opposition to our involvement in social concerns." [3]

Some groups began in 1967 to develop a more comprehensive understanding of what social investments would involve since, at that time, all the responses had been *ad hoc* ones to particular initiatives on specific issues. The 1968 General Assembly of the United Presbyterian Church mandated all of the boards under its jurisdiction to set aside thirty percent of its unrestricted funds for higher-risk, lower-return investments. The effort was begun to organize a way of making this mandate meaningful.

The earliest-published discussion of the social investment issue appears to have been Jack Mendelsohn's "Moral Concerns and Economic Strength." [4] In 1969, the Unitarian-Universalist Association published the first

[3] There are indeed some such moves. An upstate New York Conference in this executive's denomination has been struggling to develop such a policy since the fall of 1969.

[4] *Worldview,* April, 1967. A different version of this article appeared in *The Religious Situation: 1968,* ed. Donald Cutler (Boston, 1968).

pamphlet written on the subject. In it, church executive
Homer A. Jack pulled together some of the strands of
the Unitarian Church's internal discussion; it also included a Mendelsohn sermon "One Pocket or Two for
Our Cash and Our Convictions." It recounted the earlier
steps taken by the church and provided some ethical un-
derpinnings for the effort. The first systematic attempt
to link social investment to developments in the economic
and political life of the country generally and to lay a
groundwork for the various possibilities open to the investor was made in a *Christian Century* article, "Institutions, Investments, and Integrity" [5] although a shorter
piece on the same subject by Harvey Cox had appeared
in a fall, 1968 issue of *Christianity and Crisis*.

During this period, similar developments were occurring
in the foundation and university worlds. But, with the
exception of the Ford Foundation's *New Options in
the Philanthropic Process* (see chapter 2), little was
written to provide an overview of what was happening.

Then in the spring of 1969, the "Black Manifesto" of
the National Black Economic Development Conference,
led by James Forman, broke upon the churches. No
churchman could avoid confronting the issue which Forman brought to and through the doors of most of the
nation's denominations. The demand for reparations
forced the church to reconsider its total institutional activity, and the very sum demanded by the NBEDC forced

[5] *Ibid.*

the churches to look at their investment policies. Whether or not the Forman effort is successful in raising anything like the reparations demand, the impact upon the church is undeniable and the role of black churchmen in the decision-making processes of American religious institutions greatly increased. Church responses varied from contrition to revulsion, but even the most defensive responses carried a promise to think about the role of the church as an economic institution in new ways. The role of the church in the civil rights movement of the sixties had been, on balance, more aggressive than that of most American institutions. But this involvement tended to split the local church from its national boards. With the advent of Black Power, the latent hostility of many white churchmen to church involvement in the race struggle became manifest. It was the race issue which had finally paralyzed the church in the late sixties and opened up fissures within it. The Black Manifesto did not close the gaps, to be sure, but it did force the church off dead center. Once again, as had been the case a decade earlier when the church was forced to see aspects of its own institutional life (e.g. racial segregation in the congregation), the church was made to see the extent of its uncritical involvement with the society's ways. But it also discovered a key to its internal reformation and to the redefinition of its relationship to society. That key was and is the deployment of its invested assets.

One cannot divorce these developments from revelations concerning the seriousness of the threat of some industrial activities to the environment, the increasing frustration with the war effort in Southeast Asia, and consumer dissatisfaction spawned in part by seemingly runaway inflation. The disadvantaged and the disenchanted have begun to pick up support from the hitherto moderate and previously well-satisfied Americans. Serious questioning about the role of American economic institutions in the nation's life began to permeate the consciousness of not just the "radical," but the "average" man. Each of these events and many more functioned to focus greater and greater attention upon the investment policies of the churches. It is dubious that an end of the war in Vietnam, an economic recovery, or a change in national priorities will allow this door to potential social amelioration to close again. The times seem to have conspired to wedge it open for the foreseeable future.

It is impossible to be aware of, let alone summarize, the many and varied efforts of churchmen concerned about the social investment issue today. Some contrasting examples will nevertheless help convey the author's impression of the scene.

1. Churchmen with diverse social and religious viewpoints are considering a variety of ways of focusing attention upon Gulf Oil's involvement in Portuguese Angola.

2. A New York bank vice-president is leading a committee which is seeking to find ways of "circumnavigating" the prudent man rule in order to free church funds for minority economic development.

3. The Mobilization to End the War in the Churches[6] is demanding disclosure of investment holdings, wider participation in church investment decision-making, and divestment of church funds in the "military-industrial complex."

4. The United Church of Christ has recently adopted (by action of its Executive Council) a comprehensive report setting forth the Church's social investment criteria. The report bases its recommendations on its General Synod policies and examines both the various modes of social investment action and the various restraints under which church investors will work in carrying out the policy.

5. Student-based research groups from California to Boston are examining corporate activities and the relationship of church investment involvement (portfolio holdings and personnel) in those corporations whose practices they question.

6. Two major denominations, the United Presbyterians and the Episcopalians, have set task forces to work on developing social investment policies. These committees may have reported their findings by spring, 1971. Meanwhile, the Ghetto Loan and Investment Committee of the Executive Council of the Episcopalian Church and the Presbyterian Economic Development Corporation are fol-

[6] A group initiated by the People's Church Caucus, the Jonathan's Wake movement, the Submarine Church Action Network, and the Lay Movement for Responsible Renewal.

lowing their mandates to employ church investment funds in the economic development areas.[7]

7. The Massachusetts Conference of the United Church of Christ recently divested itself of one million dollars in unrestricted funds which had been functioning as endowment and turned the funds over to an ecumenical group of black churchmen.

8. The treasurer of the American Baptist Home Mission Societies has developed a social criteria proposal for his board and is seeking its acceptance by the entire board.

9. Local church investment boards have begun serious efforts to locate local or national investment opportunities in social development efforts which meet a variety of investment criteria. Churches in Chicago, New York, West Chester (Pennsylvania), New Haven, Ann Arbor, and several California cities have already made such investments.

10. A group of black churchmen and Wall Street lawyers are attempting to develop a socially responsible mutual fund, part of the profits of which will support national civil rights organizations.

11. With the precedent of the Presbyterian and National Council of Churches proxy vote for the Project on Corporate Responsibility's resolutions aimed at "making General Motors responsible," Clergy and Laymen Concerned About the War are organizing an effort to get the churches to exercise owners' rights to challenge the policies of munitions manufacturers.

[7] See discussion in chapter 4.

Introduction

12. Church pension boards, notably those of the American Baptists, the U.C.C., and the Methodists, are looking for ways to participate in the social investment movement while meeting their legal and nonlegal obligations to their pensionnaires. This is happening at a time of rising dissatisfaction with the way in which some church pension funds are managed and administered.

Two conclusions can be drawn from this sketch. One, a new consciousness is developing, both within investment committees and in the church populace generally, concerning the responsibilities of the church as investor. Two, a welter of activity is occurring at many levels and is involving many different sets of presuppositions about the rights and responsibilities of the church as investor, the nature of Christian responsibility, and the health or sickness of the nation and its processes. If funded with adequate information, motivated by adequate resolve and grass-roots support, this consciousness and the activities it is generating can make a substantive difference to the vitality, relevance, and, perhaps, the viability of the American church. The *"if"* is important, however. The issues are rarely sorted out in such a way that the presuppositional disagreements and what they entail are clear. This book represents an effort to sort out many of the issues about which there is great confusion. It has, then, its own presuppositions: clarity about the elements of and constraints upon social action initiatives will spur (and need not deter) social amelioration and effective church mission.

I
THE IMPERATIVE FOR SOCIALLY RESPONSIBLE INVESTMENT POLICIES IN THE CHURCHES

The notion of "social investment" faces a number of threshold questions. It can be argued that unless one answers them convincingly, the idea of social responsibility in investment is socially wrongheaded and even morally wrong.

Some of these "threshold" questions are the following. Will social investment policies in this economic and political system really aid the development of social justice and liberty, which were the aims of the framers of the Declaration of Independence and of the United States Constitution? Do social investment policies involve the private sector in matters which should properly be left to government and government alone? What business do nonprofit institutions have in becoming involved in such matters? Further, what is the proper role (or what are the proper roles) of the nation's churches (a specific type of nonprofit institution) in this area of social involvement? Is there any place that the church can look for guidance on the very complex moral and social questions which social investment policies will raise?

The following two chapters attempt to address these questions systematically. The first chapter is a brief history of economic and political thought and developments in this country. It explains why the writers of the Constitution handled the problem of economic life in the way they did, and then seeks to determine how well, in the subsequent evolution of the nation's economy, the values they espoused have been preserved and the mechanisms they developed have been served. This chapter concludes that, unless other ways of making or influencing economic decisions are found, including ways which involve institutions which have not traditionally been active in American economic life *per se,* the traditional goals and purposes of the nation's founders will be undermined. Economic and political histories such as this are perilous undertakings, but because the same questions are asked of the historical material throughout, the reader is helped toward the understanding of at least one perspective on that material.

The second chapter begins with a short statement about the nature and function of nonprofit institutions and briefly recounts what some nonchurch institutions are doing in the social investment field. Specific attention is then directed to the church, and an effort is made to discover whether the plurality of religious understandings of the relationship between Christians and the society in which they live provides any guidelines for developing social investment policy. The conclusion here is that the churches' self-understandings yield a clear imperative to invest with social consequences in mind, although the formulation of that imperative will differ with the "theology" of the church. Several other perspectives on the ethical questions raised by this discussion are then offered in order to specify what the church's teachings mean for social investment policy.

1
The Economic and Political Elements: An Historical Interpretation

The man who argues that in the United States there should be a relatively clear-cut distinction between the private sector (primarily business), whose chief obligations lie in spurring economic production and maximizing profit, and the public sector (the government), whose duty it is to provide for public welfare through the protection of basic constitutional rights, does not totally misunderstand the vision of the nation's founding fathers. He only misunderstands their intentions in establishing that division—and misapplies that vision to the contemporary situation.

The writers of the American Constitution had one abiding passion: that the American people would never again be *dominated,* whether by an outside power, by their own government, or by any faction or power within the country. The government was to be strong enough to resist an external invader and to assure every citizen of his civil rights. Members of the Constitutional Convention had one logistical problem, however: how does one make government strong enough to do those things without so concentrating its powers, or making it so strong, that it becomes tyrannical? The answer was twofold: to give individual states many governmental functions and to create within the central government a clear separation of powers (a system of checks and balances) among the judicial, legislative, and executive branches.

This did not mean that the writers of the Constitution intended to obliterate factions. James Madison, in initiating the Constitutional Convention, called after the Articles of the Confederation had proved too weak, made this point quite clear.

Liberty is to faction what air is to fire, an ailment without which it instantly expires. But it would not be less folly to abolish liberty, which is essential to political life, because it nourishes faction, than it would be to wish the annihilation of air because it imparts to fire its destructive activity.

Since removing the causes of factions would remove the conditions which make for liberty and its correlate, diversity, the framers of the Constitution sought instead to control its adverse *effects* in every sphere of social life.

Economic life was one of the most perplexing areas. On the one hand, the fledgling nation needed a strong, viable, and free economy if it were to survive; on the other hand, the economy could not to be so organized that within it, anymore than within the government, powerful and uncontrolled factions could dominate. Madison and his contemporaries thought that they had discovered an economic theory which would provide a way out of this potentially dangerous dilemma.

In his *Wealth of Nations* Adam Smith had persuasively argued that, if given a chance, competition among numerous producers would provide a market with the highest quality of merchandise at the lowest possible cost, while at the same time providing a living wage for the laborer. Efficiency and dynamism would be built into the life of the marketplace since, as consumer preferences changed, producers would constantly alter their products, lower their prices, improve their wage scales to compete for labor, and improve their means of production. But the invisible hand of the customer-controlled market would not only create a dynamic economy; it would also control the effects of large factions, since it would create a system so competitive that no one part of it would ever become centralized. Smith, an opponent of "big business," virtually sacralized the "self-interests" of the producer, the laborer, and the consumer, since it was man's propensity primarily to look out for himself, which would keep production dispersed and prevent monopolistic developments. Smith did not seriously entertain the proposal that a "corporation" could ever become a central or dominant factor in such an economy.

The extent to which Madison and his colleagues accepted Smith's analysis can be seen in a Madisonian speech in the First Congress (April 9, 1789):

I hold it as a truth that the commercial shackles are generally unjust, oppressive and impolitic; it is also a truth that if industry and labor are left to their own course, they will generally be directed to those objects which are the most productive, and this in a more certain and direct manner than the wisdom of the most enlightened Legislature could point out.

The principle, then, that the government and the economy which supported it should be kept separate—and that industries should be given essentially the same liberties as individuals—was thus established; not as an end in itself, but as a means to the most general end sought by the early Americans: the preservation of small but dynamic social institutions. Following the logic of this position, the Constitutional Convention made the all-important decision not to give the federal government the power to incorporate, but to allow the individual states to develop their separate corporate laws as one further check against potential monopoly and against the exercise of central governmental power.

As Henry Steele Commager has pointed out in a recent article, this decision was a clear break with the patterns established in the Old World. The Industrial Revolution in Europe took place in the context of traditionally powerful institutions: state, church, landed aristocracy, the military. Hence, business "took for granted that it occupied a subordinate and dependent position and reconciled itself to the fact that it could not have its way." [1] Rather than attempt to regulate business with (from the recent colonists' position) the all-too-visible hand of state and church, the early Americans trusted in the invisible hand of the market. The potential for developing pervasive industrial factions seemed infinitely less real than what the establishment of governmental regulation might entail. In the contemporary idiom, they decided that with respect to the economy it was better to "let it be"—which, translated, meant *laissez faire*.

In fact, practice of this theory survived for less than a quarter-century, even though most Americans are only today questioning the mythology surrounding it. In 1819 James Madison was still struggling to maintain as much of Smith's analysis as possible, while destroying its internal logic. The market had not been a sufficient impetus to stimulate industries, which the polity, through its representatives, deemed important:

There may be valuable branches of manufacture which, if once established, would support themselves, and even add to the list of exported commodities, but which, without public patronage, would either not be undertaken or come to a

[1] "America's Heritage of Bigness," *Saturday Review,* July 4, 1970, p. 10.

premature downfall. The difficulty of introducing manufactures, especially of a complicated character and costly outfit, and above all in a market preoccupied with powerful rivals, must readily be conceived. They appear, accordingly, to have required for their introduction into the countries where they are now seen in their greatest extent and prosperity, either liberal support of the Government, or the aid of exiled or emigrant manufacturers, or both of these advantages.[2]

The phrases "not be undertaken or come to a premature downfall" are not taken from Adam Smith's book; they indicate that the government learned very early that the economy would need governmental support in some of its most crucial areas and points of transition if it was to meet the needs of the nation.

The first actual break with Smith's theory came with the introduction of tariff restrictions to prevent swamping the new and struggling economy. While this could be rationalized as a way of keeping the internal market conditions stable so as to permit the market to work without interference from the outside, the succeeding steps were much harder to reconcile. Only a few years later Madison's reconstructed economic analysis became a commonplace with the transportation industry (first the canals and then the railroads), as state and federal government moved massively to spur their development.

But while government accepted the inadequacy of total

[2] Letter to Clarkson Crocius, December, 1819. *The Complete Madison: His Basic Writings,* Saul K. Padou, ed. (New York, 1953).

dependence upon the market and helped some sectors of it, it did not soon accept the correlate—that government must also regulate the market. It is true that the individual states struggled mightily to control in one single respect the already burgeoning businesses they had incorporated by limiting charter purposes. Thus, nineteenth-century lawyers spent much of their time trying to find ways for their clients to enter new fields of endeavor without going *ultra vires* (beyond their charter-given powers). Here an economic doctrine which was dependent upon industrial "smallness" (supposedly guaranteed by single-purpose charters) was pitted against what industrialization was making possible—large, multi-product industries. Economic doctrine lost, and the law of *ultra vires* became what William L. Cary has called "a social policy which failed." [3]

The nation's needs for interstate transportation not only helped bring about the demise of the "hands-off-the-economy" principle, it also made naïve and unrealistic the hope of the constitutional framers that industry in America would be primarily "intrastate." The corporations which built the great railroads with government sup-

[3] *Cases and Materials on Corporations,* 4th ed., Unabridged (Mineola, 1969), p. 359. The laws granting the states the power to incorporate served a function opposite from the intention. Rather than limit business, the states bent to serve the needs of the business community so that more money and jobs would be generated in their specific states. When one state established liberal incorporation laws, the stricter laws of the other states were rendered meaningless unless they would follow suit, for large businesses which sought more liberal incorporation laws could just change their place of incorporation to that of the more "liberal" states.

port were creating the very means by which other businesses would be able to establish national industries.

In sum, the market's invisible hand was now paralyzed because it could no longer operate upon competitive industries of limited size and location; government support of particular industries was creating outside interference; and, further, the labor demands for rapidly expanding industry helped accelerate immigration, with the end result that labor lost the bargaining position which was supposedly inherent in Smith's theory. Still, as regards regulation of product and production practices, *laissez-faire* lived on. Commager argues that the American dream of "rags to riches" prevented labor from seriously questioning the doctrine, and that the widespread acceptance of Social Darwinism, which emerged in the second half of the nineteenth century, made the successful businessman the nation's model and hero and thus hardly the man to be controlled or regulated.

Not until 1887 did the federal government use its constitutionally specified powers to "regulate commerce . . . among the several States." [4] The Interstate Commerce Commission, created by the Interstate Commerce Act, established the first regulatory agency and set the pattern which drew the national government reluctantly into its role as the visible hand, which would have to function where the invisible one no longer did. Even the Sherman anti-trust legislation sought only to prevent the "restraint of trade" by growing corporations and was accepted as a

[4] As distinct from "subsidize."

trade-off for even more restrictive tariffs. Indeed, it has never been quite clear whether federal anti-trust legislation was meant to guarantee Smith's competitive marketplace, regulate the size of economic units, or simply prevent the use of economic power contrary to the public interest as perceived by the government.[5]

Still, one should not underestimate the significance of these federal initiatives. The wedge was opened through which government moved to establish some sort of trade and industry regulation. The next thirty years (1887-1917) of American history is the story of government's slow efforts to become the visible hand controlling the deleterious effects of the increasingly powerful factions in the economic sphere. Congress enacted railroad legislation to establish equitable and competitive rates in the absence of competitive transportation alternatives; food and drug control legislation to protect the unwary consumer who could not fully protect himself, let alone control economic production; banking legislation to stabilize credit and make it more widely available to industry and individual citizens; labor legislation and judicial opinion to protect the laboring man from abuse;[6] the

[5] For example, while the Sherman Act provided for prosecution of any enterprise which restrained trade, criteria fitting both Standard Oil and U.S. Steel in the second decade of this century, only Standard Oil was prosecuted. U.S. Steel was able to argue that it had not misused its power while Standard Oil clearly left behind it not only a trail of bankrupt competitors, but public ill-feeling as well. See Grant McConnell, *Private Power and American Democracy* (New York, 1966), pp. 251-52.

[6] Labor legislation was hardly sufficient to give this "faction" an opportunity to develop into the countervailing power which Smith had

Federal Trade Commission Act, an attempt to extend regulation to nontransportation trusts involved in interstate operations.

James L. Anderson argues that, however much the increasingly powerful leaders of industry opposed these developments, they were not "a destructive attack on the existing economic system." Rather, they were designed to "correct or prevent abuses and evils" in that system and extend "democratic control over the economic system" where the factions, which were to have been self-controlled by the nature of the system in which they operated, were becoming the very type of faction that Madison and his colleagues had tried to make impossible.[7] Whereas the private-public distinction in the original scenario involved no interplay between the government and business (each inadvertently provided the requisite context in which the other could exist and fulfill its function), government found itself slowly drawn into the economic sphere—first as promoter and then as regulator—in order to allow the functions of both sectors to be fulfilled under conditions which had not earlier even been imagined.

The developments in the interaction between business and government over the last fifty years (1917–present) are much more difficult to chart chronologically. We know some of their results. The distinction between the

---

always assumed it would be when the producer bargained for laboring skills as a means to production. Judicial concern for the overextension of *federal* regulation consistently limited the scope of such legislation to enterprises involving interstate commerce (primarily the railroads).

[7] *The Emergence of the Modern Regulatory State* (Washington, D.C., 1962), pp. 155-56.

rights and responsibilities of the private and public sectors has blurred increasingly as the activities of each has intertwined with the other. Furthermore, the functions which each is called upon to perform have been greatly enlarged. The efforts of each to control the penetration of the other have been very successful at times and totally unsuccessful at others. We have witnessed the development of a pervasive and powerful government "faction," an occurrence the constitutional framers were sure they had rendered impossible, and an economy whose units are so large and whose power so centralized that Madison's dream has turned into something he would have considered a nightmare. Ownership of industry, the one assurance that the producer would think only of his own short-range self-interest (and a key to the *laissez-faire* doctrine) has been separated from the management of industry. The national resources, which seemed so absolutely unlimited in the 1800's, are now in short supply, and the effects of their utilization threaten to submerge us. American business has provided an unparalleled surfeit of goods and services. But the economic system, which was to have drawn every citizen into its cycle, excludes a large portion of the population; and the restiveness, which resulted from the disparity in life-styles spawned by that development, combined with social factors such as racial injustice, for which Smith's analysis did not begin to account, threatens domestic tranquility.[8] Further, Ameri-

---

[8] As well it might from the point of view of the ethicist concerned about such matters as distributive justice.

can business has so penetrated the economic life of every other nation that it is at once constantly sought out as the key to international development and denigrated as the imperialist influence which subverts human freedom in every part of the globe. How did we get here?

Rather than attempt an historical analysis, it is best to look separately at several of the concurrent developments just outlined.

GOVERNMENTAL POLICY

The last fifty years have witnessed a striking increase in governmental intervention in economic affairs. But one cannot understand what has happened without recognizing the important shift in government's understanding of its own responsibilities.

As noted, in the early years of the republic, protection of civil rights was considered primarily a defensive task: protection of the citizen from foreign threat, from incursion upon his freedoms by other domestic factions of the society and by other branches or units of government itself. But developments in the early part of this century, and especially after the Depression, resulted in an ever-widening conception of what constitutes public welfare. "Life, liberty, and the pursuit of happiness" were no longer seen merely as rights to be defended, but increasingly as prerogatives whose realization depends to some extent on economic and social position. As early as 1914 judicial reformer Louis Brandeis was declaring a doctrine which he spent the rest of his life supporting from the bench and which the other branches of the federal government slowly accepted: "the 'right to life' guaranteed by our Constitution is now interpreted according to the demands of social justice and of democracy as the right to *live,* not merely to exist." [9] Slowly but surely, this view was extended to apply to more and more areas of public life, and the government intervened in the economy to achieve this goal along with its others.

Whether one sees this involvement as "more of the same" type of regulation and promotion, or as policy intended to change the very character of economic and political life, the result is a "planned economy," which fits the definition of neither *laissez-faire* capitalism nor traditional socialism. It is true that in a few instances the government has assumed control of activities once in the domain of the private sector. But the TVA and Rural Electrification projects are exceptional. It does not appear at the time this book is written that the government will even choose nationalization of the ailing railroads (particularly the Penn-Central) as the option to support slumping land transportation services.[10] Nor does the experiment of the sixties in joint government-industry ownership (e.g., the consortium created by the Communications

[9] Anderson, *The Emergence of the Modern Regulatory State,* p. 79.

[10] Even though the federal government's constitutionally granted powers are clearest in regulating interstate commerce. See John Kenneth Galbraith, "Who Needs the Democrats?" *Harper's Magazine,* July 1970, pp. 43-62, for an argument in favor of governmental ownership of specified industries.

Satellite Act of 1962) appear to have become the model for the future, although it is perhaps too soon to tell.[11]

Instead, government has constantly explored new options for federal subsidy and regulation. The results are not always happy, nor, as most persons recognize, adequate. The most active programs for public subsidy have continued in the fields of transportation, agriculture, and defense.

The rider on the Penn-Central often boards a railroad car owned by a governmental agency and leased to the railroad. Subsidies of a bewildering variety support farm prices, and the size of individual grants are just now coming under effective limitation. The federal government owns and leases much of the means of production of privately owned and governed Lockheed, the nation's number one defense producer. Indeed, many of the initiatives in economic regulation come in the form of what are in effect subsidies (tax incentives, for example).

In the field of direct regulation, too, the government has struggled to navigate the straits between "control" and "free enterprise." As we have seen, regulatory agencies came into being when it appeared that the effects of certain businesses needed some regulation by some governmental branch.[12] For example, the Interstate Commerce Commission was created during the era of intense

[11] The National Corporation for Housing Partnerships discussed in chapter 4 is a recent example, however.

[12] The agencies were at first organized with lines of accountability directly to the Congress: as that form of organization proved inefficient, some administrative agencies were established with regulatory

railroad rate competition when the giants charged the user exorbitantly after driving smaller competitors out of business. The Federal Trade Commission restrained industrial giants who controlled the market, and later made recommendations in anti-trust cases.

On behalf of the public the agencies were to regulate industry by making rules which had the force of law and by adjudicating disputes in their area. They became independent centers of administrative, legislative, and judicial power. Then, as their power was formalized, as Commission members developed empathy with the problems of those corporations they were to regulate, and as their procedures became increasingly judicial, their activity on behalf of the public waned.[13]

The point here is not that government regulation is wrong, that it is always ineffective, or that it always carries out policies contrary to public interest. Regulatory agencies are just not equivalent to Smith's invisible hand. As

---

functions which were accountable directly to the President. Regulatory agency procedures, or lines of accountability, have always been confusing. The legislative or executive branch first gave the agencies broad mandates and later specific grievances to examine. Lacking sufficient funds to carry out their broad mandate, they often tended to concentrate on the more picayune matters, losing sight of their intended broad purposes.

[13] This development was spurred by the Administrative Procedures Act of 1946, which, in attempting to regularize agency procedures, helped turn them into independent judicatories to which both plaintiffs and defendants had to come with equally well-prepared briefs —a strange style of activity for a watch-dog body. Philip Elman, a Federal Trade Commissioner for nine years, has recently called for changes which would remove judicial powers from regulatory agency mandates and permit them to become advocates again.

it has developed, regulation has brought along with it a decline of many public interest suits. (Witness the decline of anti-trust prosecution in the past twenty years as corporations accumulated great economic and productive interests.)

The Hoover Commission, President Kennedy, and other observers of regulatory commissions affirmed John Kenneth Galbraith's observation of 1955:

Regulatory bodies, like the people who comprise them, have a marked life-cycle. In youth they are vigorous, aggressive, evangelistic, and even intolerant. Later they mellow, and in old age—after a matter of ten or fifteen years—they become, with some exceptions, either an arm of the industry they are regulating or senile.[14]

It is important to note one other type of federal action —that which supports weak nongovernmental associations, thus permitting them to become additional sources of countervailing power against an increasingly concentrated economic sector. The most striking example is in the field of labor law. The original legislation in this field was intended primarily to improve the laborer's wages and

[14] *The Great Crash* (New York, 1955), p. 171; or as more recently seen in a case involving the Securities and Exchange Commission, in which the District of Columbia Circuit of the U.S. Court of Appeals criticized that body for supporting the interests of those they regulated rather than interests of those in whose behalf they were established and argued that the S.E.C. had failed to make available to a non-industry plaintiff "the potential benefit of the Commission's resources and expertise as an ally in compliance litigation" against the company in question. See *Medical Committee for Human Rights* v. *Securities Exchange Commission,* July 8, 1970.

working conditions.[15] The corollary principle of assuring the wage earner's right to join with his fellows has always been part of the intention of some governmental offices. As early as 1914 Woodrow Wilson spoke of the need for congressional guarantees of the union's "right to organize." This principle was first applied to railroad workers in 1926 legislation, and in the New Deal, especially in the National Labor Relations Act, it was applied more forcefully and broadly. The 1964 Civil Rights Act, establishing the Equal Employment Opportunity Commission, is an important and recent example. Although the federal government has been aware of the potential dangers of labor power, government regulation has not necessarily been any more effective in striking a balance in this field than it has been in industrial regulation. But the government did tacitly accept the need to become the visible hand in the "labor" part of Adam Smith's equation.

The government has also bolstered the potential power of the stockholder group. In 1933 and 1934 Congress responded to some of the causes of the Great Crash of 1929 by adopting two laws relating to securities. Stock purchase until this time had often been a highly risky, speculative affair, with virtually no guarantees that the pur-

[15] One brief set of statistics will suggest how much this was needed. Between 1860 and 1890 the nation's wealth increased 500 percent, but in one decade within that thirty-year period (1870's), real income declined from an average of $400 to $300, although the working man was struggling valiantly to improve his situation. Between 1881 and 1894, for example, there were 14,000 strikes involving four million workers. See J. Milton Yinger, *The Scientific Study of Religion* (New York, 1970).

chaser could count on regularized stock purchase procedures, would know the strength of the companies of which he was becoming part-owner, or would be protected from irregular procedures by knowing precisely for what he was voting as a shareholder. Though some of this sounds like consumer-protection legislation, it also possessed, at least as the courts have recently interpreted congressional intent, a concept of corporate democracy which would help provide for informed stockholder influence in the basic practices of corporations. This regulation's intent was to prohibit the "control of great corporations," obviously the key economic unit, from coming into the hands of "a very few persons" (e.g., *S. E. C.* v. *Transamerica Corp.*, U.S. Court of Appeals, Third Circuit, 1947) with massive power. In these and other ways, government has attempted to maintain a plurality of "factions" which have power to affect the flow of events.

CORPORATE DEVELOPMENT

Ironically, as Congress was passing the securities legislation, Adolph Berle and Gardiner Means in their *Modern Corporation and Private Power* were documenting two important conclusions about the American economy: two hundred American corporations had obtained control of almost fifty percent of the nation's industrial corporate wealth;[16] but the control of those assets had clearly

[16] The trend toward concentration and its corollary, corporate diversification, has clearly continued; in 1967 Berle concluded that

shifted from their "owners" (the stockholders) to their managers (executives and the board of directors). This conclusion, virtually uncontested today, is reiterated in the writings of thinkers as different as Edward S. Mason, John Kenneth Galbraith, and C. Wright Mills. The extent to which we will accept as desirable Berle's view of the stockholder as "passive-receptive" will be the subject of the remainder of the book. But, as things now stand (or at least stood until recent months), the legally sanctioned proposal that the corporation exists "for the benefit of the stockholder" is a legal fiction.[17]

For whom does it exist, if not for the stockholder? In one way or another, for the managers—although this assertion must be put in perspective. The managerial revolution is germane to our discussion in several ways. First, it undermines the view that the corporation exists to maximize profit. The corporation has become an institution, intended by its managers to exist in perpetuity. In such a situation, the long-range self-interest of the *corporation* (as the manager's future employer and as his "achievement" *vis-à-vis* the other economic units in the society) becomes the guiding passion of the manager. The

---

"today half of the nation's manufacturing assets are held by 150 companies." See "Economic Power and the Free Society," *Fund for the Republic Pamphlets,* December, 1967.

[17] If, indeed, it was more than that at any time for anyone except the great entrepreneurs. In the first decade of the century, stock turnover rates often reached 200 percent, hardly an indication that the shareholder saw himself in the role of the producer-manager. See Robert Sobel, *The Big Board* (New York, 1965), p. 159.

emergence of the management-controlled corporation, then, brings the final disintegration of Adam Smith's model. No longer can the market make or break a corporation; some divisions do well some years, supporting those which do not. All this fits hand in glove with most government purposes: there are larger and more stable units to regulate, fewer constituencies to control, and more dependable production methods in businesses from which the government procures its goods and services, and obtains its taxes.

None of this is necessarily counter to the interests of the common man. He benefits from the increased availability of goods and services, from a relatively more stable but growing economy, and from an economy in which every major component tends to act in the long-range interests of all whom its cycle includes. It is only harmful to those who do not participate in the most dynamic parts of the cycle or to those whom it abuses. And it troubles those concerned that the exercise of power be legitimated and that the society be assured that those who have the ability to turn the economy off and on at various points are accountable to the wider society. What happens when the long-range interest of corporate America capriciously leaves some citizens out of the picture? Gone is the legitimacy which that magical market was going to guarantee; and its proposed replacement, the visible hand of the government—either legitimated by the source of its appointment (ultimately by the electorate) or by its existence as a countervailing power—has never effectively assumed that role.[18]

Economic historians, politicians, and the corporate managers themselves have not overlooked these developments. As early as 1933, Louis Brandeis urged business to become "a new profession," for professions have traditionally conceived themselves as composed of persons whose power to control the lives of others is justified only because they act in the interest of those they affect and are monitored by equally public-spirited peers. The contemporary crisis of management—which is essentially a crisis of legitimacy—has yielded countless executive tracts on corporate social responsibility which assert one of two interrelated propositions: that the long-range self-interest of the corporation (whose manager is the custodian) is virtually synonymous with the self-interest of the society at large; or, and this is the final irony for the American system, that the corporation exists first of all "for the well-being of society"—period.[19] As suggested in Appendix A, it is unclear as yet whether this is a rhetorical flourish to cover a multitude of past sins and to justify the exercise of future power which otherwise would be unacceptable, or whether it truly is a shift in the very purpose and goals of what have previously been economic units only.

But will such shifts, defined and controlled by management, be sufficient? The answer which the populace gives

[18] Again, Commager's historical explanation for this, cited earlier in the *Saturday Review* article, seems on target.

[19] See p. 186 of this book.

to this question depends on two factors: (1) what goes on in the plant, in the executive suite, and in the corporation foundation, *ad infinitum,* to provide warrants for the use of "responsibility" language; and (2) the extent to which the general view of the American people of what constitutes their "well-being" coheres with the view articulated by the manager. The central point here, however, is that, with the shift in corporate self-definition, a revolution in economic theory has occurred, and any attempt to maintain the constitutional framers' insistence upon civil liberties and individual rights will have to recognize that the nation has created or allowed to be created an economy functioning in a manner wholly different from that which those framers envisioned.

In sum, talk today of a clear private-public distinction, at least as regards the business-government relationship, fails to read history's signposts. Somewhere along the way these two streams have almost merged and their identities have became blurred. At the same time that each of those sectors has expanded the responsibilities specified in their original mandates, they have come to overlap so completely that they are neither formally nor materially separable. On the one hand, through regulative agencies, government has become the chief economic planner—largely with the blessings of the nation's giant corporations. Persuasive or forceful government action on many fronts (e.g., as procurer) determines primarily where and when economic growth or decrease takes place. On the other hand, the economic sector has, again more informally than formally, taken over what were once clearly government functions. As Edward Mason puts it in his introduction to *The Corporation in Modern Society:*

Government has sought increasingly to use the private corporations for the performance of what are essentially public functions. Private corporations, in turn, particularly in their foreign operations, continually make decisions which impinge on the public—particularly foreign—policy of government.[20]

It is strange, but not necessarily "bad," that both business and government leaders acknowledge and applaud this fact. Industry and government should work "not as adversaries, but as allies," James Roche, Chairman of the Board of General Motors, has said.[21] One of the primary themes of a book by James Tobin, a member of President Kennedy's Council of Economic Advisers, is suggested by his chapter, "The New Era of Good Feeling Between Business and Government." [22]

In such a situation there are basically two questions to ask, even before we attempt to figure out where to go from here:

[20] (Cambridge, Mass., 1959), p. 16. In a speech in 1965 to the Society of Automotive Engineers, Lynn Townsend, President of the Chrysler Corporation, pointed out that U.S. corporations invested $4.3 billion outside the country, approximately twice as much as the U.S. government's expenditures outside the country for economic foreign aid in that year.

[21] Speech to Illinois Manufacturer's Association, Chicago, Illinois, December 12, 1968.

[22] *National Economic Policy* (New Haven, Conn., 1966).

The Economic and Political Elements

1. What is being done for those who are still left out of the eco-political system described here? With or without inflation, minor recessions, and bearish stock markets, the real income level of most Americans continues to rise. Yet, the disparity between the incomes and life-styles of the very rich and the very poor continues to grow.

2. What is the long-range prospect for civil freedoms in a nation, established with the goal of maintaining liberty by means of keeping all its institutions small and pluralistic, but which has evolved several highly concentrated centers of power (government, business, and perhaps labor) and then has allowed the line of demarcation between those power centers to become blurred, if not expunged?

There is no paucity of proposals. Some promise answers to both of these questions through "decentralization," although there are few realistic suggestions which explain how those who control the massive centers of power will be persuaded to pass their power around, except as regards peripheral aspects of the nation's life. Some want to reassert a fairly clear-cut public-private distinction, although this is precisely what many expected to happen with the emergence of the regulatory state and it did not. Some argue that the one option this nation has never tried is socialism, although, as John Kenneth Galbraith points out, government's slice of the economic pie in this country is already larger than that of such "socialist" economies as Sweden's, Norway's, and is not far behind Poland's.[23] Furthermore, socialism hardly represents less

[23] *The New Industrial State* (Boston, 1967), p. 15.

concentrated (although admittedly a more easily legitimated) power. Some suggest, and the judicial branch increasingly seems to support the view, that corporations ought to be treated as "states" and made subject to the same rules, such as due-process and fair and equal treatment of those affected.[24] Others suggest that all the concern is unnecessary because, since the managerial revolution the once supposedly "soulless" corporation has discovered that it too can have soul, and that one can trust to adequate expressions of conscience as well.[25] But one must be wary of (an ethicist especially worries about) making the future of a people or the world depend on the hope that a few corporate consciences may become sensitized. Indeed, if there is any lesson still to be learned from Madison, it is this one.

In sum, we do not yet have an adequate paradigm or theory for the economic and political life of contemporary America, and we surely do not yet know how to move from the present situation to that new form. The framers of the Constitution thought they had one, and perhaps one of the impediments to our ability to find a new one is that the paradigm of the past so haunts us that we use it selectively to justify some pieces of our present eco-

[24] Kingman Brewster, "The Corporation and Economic Federalism," in *The Corporation in Modern Society,* ed. Edward Mason; and Arthur Selwyn Miller, "The Constitution and the Voluntary Association: Some Notes Toward a Theory," in *Voluntary Associations,* ed. John W. Chapman, seem to suggest such an alternative.

[25] Adolph Berle appears to move toward this view in his "Economic Power and the Free Society," *Fund for the Republic Pamphlets,* December, 1967.

nomic and political life even though it doesn't fit most of the puzzle. Some of the suggestions just noted may well be elements in the new paradigm.

But Edward Mason correctly summarizes the present state of affairs:

The fact seems to be that the rise of the large corporation and attending circumstances have confronted us with a long series of questions concerning rights and duties, privileges and immunities, responsibility and authority, that political and legal philosophy have not yet assimilated. What we need among other things is a twentieth century Hobbes or Locke to bring some order to our thinking about the corporation and its role in society.[26]

Social investment represents neither such a philosophy nor a sure means to finding it. It does represent—and this is all that this book claims for it—a middle-range proposal for beginning to deal with some of the problems that a "theory-less" political economy is creating. At the same time it is a way of putting a wide variety of inputs into that system so that the options for a free society, in Brandeis' words, which allow people to "live," not merely "exist," are not foreclosed before that new theory or paradigm emerges.

[26] *The Corporation in Modern Society,* p. 19.

2
The Ecclesiastical and Theological Elements: The Churches and the Non-Profit Sector

Recent discussion about the demise of American pluralism has focused on two quite separable points, one descriptive and one normative:

(1) that the concentration of social power proceeds apace; it is precisely this point which the previous chapter has attempted to demonstrate; and

(2) that this development is somehow automatically good in a technological society; it is this argument which the author has been less willing to accept.

The Ecclesiastical and Theological Elements

In the introduction to his *Decline of American Pluralism,* Henry S. Kariel declares: "I would have us move, if this be possible, from the much celebrated ideal of de Tocqueville toward the still unfashionable one of Rousseau, from a hierarchical public order toward an equalitarian one." [1] He rightly points out that many, if not most, of the institutions in our private sector are hierarchically, even oligarchically, governed, and he, along with many others, calls for the development of "democratic constitutionalism" as the form of government in the private sector.[2]

Clearly, this is the end toward which many Americans, especially those under thirty, would like to move. But here, means-ends questions are raised. For Madison and his contemporaries pluralism was not an end; it was the means to liberty. Madison's world is gone—but that is all the more reason for not throwing the baby out with the bathwater as we search for the means to liberty and justice in the contemporary period. However murky the water, it will have to be let out with some care. Not until some reasonable assurance exists that there have been established both adequate processes for accountability and truly acceptable patterns of responsibility in the massive power centers we have described, do fitful moves toward the dismemberment of other possible sources of countervailing power in this society make good social sense.

In a concurring opinion to the Supreme Court's 1968

[1] (Stanford, 1961), p. 4.
[2] For example, Sanford Lakoff, "Private Government in the Managed Society," *Voluntary Associations,* ed. John W. Chapman (New York, 1969).

decision, giving the taxpayer standing in the courts to challenge certain patterns of government spending, Justice William O. Douglas made this point clear in regard to government, although it might equally well be made in regard to corporate enterprise:

The Constitution . . . is not adequate to protect the individual against the growing bureaucracy in the Legislative and Executive branches. He faces a formidable opponent in government, even when he is endowed with funds and with courage. The individual is almost certain to be plowed under unless he has a well-organized active political group to speak for him. The church is one, the press is another, the union is a third. But if a powerful sponsor is lacking, individual liberty withers—in spite of glowing opinions and resounding constitutional phrases.[3]

What are these sources of countervailing power and organized social action? Potentially there are many, but perhaps the most important are the institutions which constitute the private nonprofit sector, including churches, foundations and universities. (There are other types of nonprofit organizations, including unions and chambers of commerce; here we focus on charitable institutions.) These institutions gain strength in part through their tax-exempt status and are mandated to pursue the welfare of their members or those they affect, within the scope of their declared purposes, but in a manner only broadly

[3] *Flast* v. *Cohen,* 392, U.S. 83, 102 (1968).

indicated by government. On the one hand, their perquisites are justified because they "bear burdens that would otherwise either have to be met by general taxation or be left undone to the detriment of the community"; on the other hand, on the basis we have been discussing: "each group [in the nonprofit sector] contributes to the diversity of association, viewpoint, and enterprise essential to vigorous pluralistic society."

As we suggested earlier, blurring the public-private distinction creates two main areas of concern:

(1) those left outside the political-economic cycle are often left bereft of either advocates or support; and

(2) groups with sufficient influence to affect the practices within that cycle tend to monitor them less adequately, should these practices be socially deleterious.

Although there are many ways in which the nonprofit sector has responded and should continue to respond to these two concerns, our concern here is primarily with their relationship to investment practices.

Economically speaking, nonprofit institutions are strange hybrids. They generally receive their funds from tax-deductible contributions. Although exceptions exist, their income is tax-deductible and their real property is exempt. Their expenditures fall within categories adjudged to be in the public interest. What is omitted from this cycle of nonprofit finance is: (1) the investments which such institutions make in the private profit sector to increase and sustain their financial worth; and (2) the purchases they make from that sector. Although we will examine some exceptions, these institutions in general have invested their wealth with the sole purpose of gaining the highest possible return for their programs and have, like any housewife, sought the lowest-priced quality commodities in their procurement practices.

While investing and purchasing were never morally and socially neutral, the nonprofit sector's separation of its fund-accumulation and fund-deployment procedures was partially justifiable as long as a relatively clear-cut distinction existed between the responsibilities of the private profit sector (profit and economic growth) and the public sector (public equity and welfare). However, the breakdown of the public-private distinction, discussed in the previous chapter, suggests the need for qualifying, if not obliterating, the division of their houses between investments and expenditures assumed by charitable institutions.

If that separation continues, we will witness the strange (indeed anomalous) situation in which the private, profit-making business sector includes "public equity and welfare" as one of its responsibilities, while some of its charitably oriented "owners" continue to view the corporation simply as a source of revenue derived from profits. It would seem axiomatic that these nonprofit institutions should be providing the leadership, direction, and expert opinion on how the total society must organize itself to solve the social issues and problems which today are growing like Topsy. Because of their power and their experience, these institutions should be leading other investors (personal trust fund fiduciaries and mutual fund directors, for example) to think in new and longer-range ways about what is involved in serving the ultimate interests of their beneficiaries and clients, whomever they may be.[4]

Three quite separate points are being made here, but all lead in the same direction:

(1) to the extent that private nonprofit institutions participate in the private-profit sector to increase their wealth, they should use their invested wealth to obtain social ends, at least to the extent that profit-making institutions in the private sector do;

(2) because the nonprofit sector obtained its tax-exempt status by reason of serving the public good, it has a greater responsibility than the business sector to utilize its total resources (and not simply its investment *yield*) for those public purposes; and

(3) since nonprofit institutions are by definition in the business of promoting some aspect of public welfare, not profit, they presumably are better prepared to know what is required to ameliorate social ills than are corporations, which are just now organizing themselves for the task. This knowledge should serve to make

[4] In suggesting this, I am aware of the variety of often restrictive legal obligations under which fiduciaries of various types of trusts now operate. Extended discussion of some of these will be given in chapter 5.

them especially competent in the use of their investments as well as in the use of their yield for social purposes.

At long last, movement in this direction is beginning. The Introduction has offered a brief analysis of church initiatives. Here we will mention some of the efforts being made by foundations and universities. In 1967 the Ford Foundation, spurred by the Taconic Foundation and joined by others (including New World, Field, Norman, and Rockefeller Brothers) announced a change in its policy which made investment policy part of its philanthropic program.[5] The Ford Foundation, for example, hopes to increase the impact of its giving by making higher-risk, lower-return investments to minority businesses and housing and conservation projects.[6] How much this experiment will become a basic mode of foundation operation and whether it will lead foundations as stockholders to persuade corporations to adopt more responsible practices is not yet clear. At about the same time that foundations took these steps, a variety of initiatives on university campuses, including Princeton, Cornell, Antioch, Stanford, Yale, Harvard, Union Theological Seminary, and Brown, raised the social investment issue for educational institutions with varying degrees of success. A monograph on university investment policy, growing out of an inter-

[5] A Ford Foundation pamphlet, *New Options in the Philanthropic Process,* obtainable through the Foundation's offices, 320 East Forty-third Street, New York, N.Y. 10017, best describes this initiative.

[6] The Cooperative Assistance Fund, initiated primarily by Taconic, will serve as a primary vehicle for some of these operations.

disciplinary course, "Yale's Investments" at Yale University, attempts to analyze the variety of problems (including academic neutrality) which these proposals raise, and proposes a specific policy.[7] Many of these institutions faced one aspect of the problem last spring when asked to vote for or against a proposal for corporate reform made by "Project GM" (now the Project on Corporate Responsibility) to General Motors stockholders.[8] It is essential to recognize that the public service responsibilities of nonprofit institutions differ; some are more restricted in their sphere of operations than others. Foundation corporate charters, for example, generally allow greater latitude than do the charters of educational institutions;[9] but one thing is certain: "It is increasingly clear that there is going to be more concern with social conscience in the investment decision unless we are to go back to the cave age."[10]

And what about the churches? We have seen some of what they are doing; the question here is what should they be doing?

In exhorting American churches to take on the new responsibility we have suggested, one is tempted to shift into one of two modes of argument:

[7] This document will soon be published by John G. Simon, Jon P. Gunnemann, and the author.

[8] See chapter 4 for a fuller discussion of this effort.

[9] Ford's purpose, for example, is to advance the "public welfare."

[10] J. Richardson Dilworth, chairman of the Finance Committee of the Yale Corporation, Yale University, as quoted in "Do Institutional Investors Have a Social Responsibility?" in the *Institutional Investor*, July, 1970, p. 30.

(1) to assume a critical and sociological stance and recite the persistent failure of the American church to lead the society toward the new and dynamic change which is required. Such an approach would castigate the church as a slothful defender of the *status quo* in a desperate attempt to awaken the religious conscience; (2) to launch an all-embracing theological justification with a specific imperative for church action—recalling biblical passages and pointing to pieces of the ecclesiastical tradition as the justification for a particular theological point of view.

These two arguments share the assumption that religion in America is or should be monolithic. But historical and sociological evidence suggests that American churches have been and are a variety of things: centers of recalcitrance and apology for societal indolence; symbol-makers for important new thrusts in societal mores, morals, and structures; and, most often, wayside inns for bystanders who want to step aside from complex cultural developments and wait out the storm. On the theological side, the churches house a variety of basic views concerning the way in which religious men and institutions should relate to their culture, and within each of these are different views on specific issues.

How does one take both aspects of this heterogeneity into account and still argue for a whole new style of church financial thinking and management, informed both by the changing economic and political patterns in society and by a serious reexamination of the ecclesiastical self-understanding? However difficult, that is the task set for us in the remainder of this chapter. Indeed, we will be arguing that changing institutional patterns and the corresponding need for the development of social investment policies in nonprofit institutions could be the issue through which the churches and churchmen will find their true nature, and hence find the points of real (not simply expedient) commonality and real (not simply expedient) diversity which exist among them.

What is the basis for this assertion? As long as the church followed other nonprofit institutions in distinguishing between asset-generating and program-spending funds, its efforts to find an integrated and consistent ethic applicable to the whole institution were bound to founder. In his important "Reparations: A Call to Repentance," Max Stackhouse relates to the specific crisis in the church created by the *Black Manifesto,* a more general point which he has been attempting to make about the institutional church for some time:

To be a viable institution there must be an inner logic, a *raison d'être,* a claim to legitimacy which invests its network of relationships with noncoercive power and with a sense of worth. . . . No institutional force can sustain itself organizationally without a claim to embody value and purpose at its very center, in its inwardness. These core values and purposes are the spirituality of institutions and determine the "will" of the organization.[11]

[11] "Reparations: A Call to Repentance," *Renewal,* June, 1969, pp. 4-5. It should be noted here that it is precisely such a *raison d'être* which the modern corporation lacks in contemporary America. See Appendix A.

The urgent need for churches as nonprofit institutions to begin employing their wealth in ways consistent with their call to expend time, energy, and program money to the glory of God and the benefit of man can be the occasion in which that inner logic (or what might be called institutional integrity) will show itself and will invest the entire network of the churches' relationships with a sense of worth. Historians and sociologists will not be sanguine about the possibility;[12] while Christian ethicists should not be as naïve as they often have been, they should never despair. As already hinted, the danger now is to move too quickly and prematurely toward a single definition of what should be that "inner logic" of the Christian's responsibility in, and to, culture.[13]

In his classic typology of Christianity's diverse understandings of the relationship of faith to culture, *Christ and Culture,* H. Richard Niebuhr isolated five different views. Each has its own enduring sources in the Western tra-

[12] See Jeffrey Hadden, *The Gathering Storm in the Churches* (New York, 1968); Milton Yinger, *The Social Scientific Study of Religion* (New York, 1970); Joseph Hough, *Black Power and White Protestants* (New York, 1968); Pierre Berton, *The Comfortable Pew* (Philadelphia, 1965); Gerhard Lenski, *The Religious Factor: A Sociologist's Inquiry* (New York, 1961); Liston Pope, *Millhands and Preachers* (New Haven, 1942); Kenneth Underwood, *Protestant and Catholic* (Boston, 1957).

[13] In the article noted above, Stackhouse makes this move (a mistaken one, from the author's point of view) by calling for a new, all-embracing "social theology" which seems to amount to an updaded 'Social Gospel" theology. As the ecumenical movement has discovered, a common theology, especially in this period of cultural diffusion, is probably the final and not the initial area in which commonality will be found.

dition, its own understanding of the biblical message, its own precedents in American church history, its own denominational examples, and, one should stress, its own inner logic and integrity. Obviously, within each of these types are importantly different theological views; obviously, each of the five views has been affected by and has itself affected cultural developments; further, many American churches have lost touch with their own historical roots and hold on to the shell rather than the substance of them. Still, if churchmen and churches can, through the medium of this typology, isolate where they mean their church to be standing in relation to society, then they may be able to rediscover or reaffirm what "inner logic" should be driving their church and better comprehend what the key principles of their social investment policies should be. We shall look at each of these views separately and suggest broad implications for investment policy.

CHRIST OF CULTURE

We must reduce our volume to the simple Evangelists; select even from them the very words of Jesus, paring off the amphilogisms into which they have been led, by forgetting often, or not understanding, what had fallen from Him, by giving their own misconceptions as His dicta, and expressing unintelligibly for others what they had not understood themselves. There will be found remaining the most sublime and benevolent code of morals which ever has been offered to man.

—Thomas Jefferson, in a letter to John Adams (1813)[14]

One view of Christianity serves primarily to sacralize the existing culture. It is often referred to as cultural religion; H. Richard Niebuhr calls it the "Christ of culture" view.[15] The figure of Christ here is generally that of a "wise man teaching a secular wisdom," although *which wisdom* depends very much upon what ideal the particular culture espouses. The view makes some distinctions between the performance of various cultures, but it holds to the basic faith that the evolution of society's response to various pressures (including economic ones) will be generally consistent with what Christianity demands. It finds no great tension (at least none which is expected to endure) between the church and the world. Since culture is interpreted through Christ, and Christ is interpreted through culture, cultural aberrations, where perceived, are always considered remediable. Niebuhr points out that since it exists without a really stable reference point, this type of Christianity becomes chameleon-like, and appeal to "Christ" always risks being nothing more than "an honorific and emotional term" by which the church attaches a "numinous quality to its personified

---

[14] I am indebted to James M. Gustafson's *Christ and the Moral Life* (New York, 1968), p. 195, for this quote.

[15] Albrecht Ritschl, Thomas Jefferson, and Abraham Lincoln are representative theologians of this view of Christianity.

ideals." [16] The ethical task in this view is to "realize and conserve" the values already operative in the society, although in a society whose values are as diverse and diffuse as this one's are, it is bold to anticipate whose flag one will be carrying.[17]

Implications for Investments. From the point of view of churches embracing this definition of Christianity, the "integrity" required of the investing church seeks to promote the best evolving values and practices in the existing economic system. It will tend to ignore pressures for extraordinary alterations in business practice and the calls for support among those who propose economic options importantly different from existing ones. This does not mean that its proponents will not seek an economy in better accord with the principles of equality and distributive justice; it does mean that these will not normally be pursued through any means which will "rock the boat," since the boat is already in the right channel.

CHRIST AGAINST CULTURE

Do not love the world or the things in the world. If any one loves the world, love for the Father is not in him.

—I John 2:15

[16] *Christ and Culture* (New York, 1951), p. 107.

[17] This understanding of Christianity is the target of more serious theological and biblical objections than any of the others. See Niebuhr, pp. 108-15.

At the opposite end of the spectrum is the "Christ against culture" view. This view, which has normally been represented institutionally in the religious tradition by sects and sectarian movements, avers that the Christian faith leads to a *rejection* of the ways in which the rest of society operates. The ways of culture are viewed as so alien to the way of relating Christ to personal and institutional practice that the only possible Christian response is to withdraw entirely from that society and establish another "culture" based upon a new standard of behavior—normally developed from one of several rigorous and unmitigated readings of biblical, and especially New Testament precepts which the faith has made available and possible. Always implicit here is an optimism that such new communities will work and that a new style of life is attainable if only one can break away from the institutional structures which have mired men down in the "old" culture.

Implications for Investment. The inner logic of this way of relating faith to culture suggests that such a church will not maintain investments in the economic marketplace of the old culture—their concerns for economic and social justice would apply only to the culture they have newly created. The Mennonite Church's response to a recent letter about its investment policy reflects the dilemma of a "sectarian" movement whose membership is reestablishing contact with the larger community while attempting to hold on to the religious values which had sustained its life apart (a development experienced by most sects in the past) :

> We have been rurally oriented. We are good farmers. We have demonstrated considerable ability in making good investments in some of the best farmland. . . . Mennonites are [however] rapidly becoming urbanized. . . . So, we are being pushed more and more into the common economic community. And only within the past several years have we confronted the matter of Christian ethics as they concern the employment of financial resources. In rethinking our investment guidelines, we are becoming aware of the numerous conflicts to the Christian as he attempts to put his money to work.[18]

It is quite clear that the integrity, the inner logic, of the "Christ-culture" relationship which this church has maintained in the past will inform its practice in the changed situation.

CHRIST AND CULTURE IN PARADOX

> For while we are still in this [earthly] tent, we sigh with anxiety; . . . we know that while we are at home in the body we are away from the Lord.—II Corinthians 5:4, 6

And Jesus said to them, "Whose likeness and inscription is this?" They said, "Caesar's." Then he said to them, "Ren-

---

[18] Letter to the author from John H. Rudy, Director of Financial Services, The Mennonite Foundation, 111 Marilyn Ave., Goshen, Ind.

der to Caesar the things that are Caesar's, and to God the things that are God's."—Matthew 22:20-21

Christians holding this view are as despairing about the redeemability of culture as are those who hold the previous view, but they are more thoroughgoing in their despair. The problem is not in the "old" structures and institutions which might be changed, but in man himself. They therefore remain a part of culture, but believe that the demands of Christianity upon the church and its members are virtually unattainable. The requirements of Christianity and the mores of culture are paradoxically related and create a dualism of responsibilities. Those who organize culture (government, leaders of the economy), many of whom are to be Christians themselves, are given great authority, not because they are doing it "right," but because in this world everyone will do it "wrong." Sometimes, however, religious obedience is nearly equated with obedience to those who direct the society, since they are, albeit in imperfect ways, the "mask of God" in this imperfect world.

Implications for Investment. It does not follow that those Christians who espouse this view will not or should not develop a social investment policy; it does follow that in its investments, as in its programs, such a church will adopt canons of responsibility similar to those of other sectors of society. For example, churches guided by this view will find it as appropriate as the "Christ of culture" churches to make their social investment policies consistent with those of the universities, foundations, and other charitable institutions. Again, however, the inner logic of this understanding of Christianity requires this, not because these initiatives will represent Christian ideals, but because Christian ideals cannot work in this world.

CHRIST ABOVE CULTURE

Think not that I have come to abolish the law and the prophets; I have come not to abolish them but to fulfil them.
—Matthew 5:17

Like the "Christ and culture in paradox" view, this one holds that man has not the power to inculcate the highest ideals of the faith into his cultural life. Faith, hope, and love are norms and virtues of Christians which institutional practice rarely expresses. But these Christians are more sanguine than the previous type about (1) their ability to create a culture which will serve the *societal* needs of man; and (2) the possibility, albeit it is no more than that, that individual Christians have the capacity to go "the extra mile" to attain truly Christian ideals in personal relationships—if rarely in societal ones. In this way the view discussed here moves toward the "Christ of culture" position, but always maintains a transcendent set of principles by which it judges the existing society. Thomas Aquinas, Niebuhr suggests, is the theologian whose view of the faith best accords with this one.

Implications for Investment. As with the last two "types" discussed, this view of the faith-culture relationship points toward an investment policy which relies heavily upon the norms evolving in the economic life of the society at large. But it has an added dimension. The "Christ above culture" Christian is never satisfied with his society; he is always seeking to help it approximate more closely his faith's "transcendent" ideals. Furthermore, he always tests every existing social arrangement or effort to change it against those ideals. He never expects great strides to be made; nor is he fundamentally pessimistic about the possibilities of existing culture meeting earthly needs. This will be reflected in the way he approaches the persuasion of corporate America as well as the way in which he seeks to help those who have been left out of political and economic life in his investment policies. He will not laud culture; but neither does he disparage it.

CHRIST TRANSFORMING CULTURE

For God sent the Son into the world, not to condemn the world, but that the world might be saved through him.
—John 3:17

God was in Christ reconciling the world to himself, not counting their trespasses against them, and entrusting to us the message of reconciliation.—II Corinthians 5:19

It is the fifth view of Christ and culture which most, but not all, contemporary "mainline" American denominations seem to hold in their theological affirmations and pronouncements. Niebuhr calls this the "Christ-transforming culture" type. Here the Christian does not simply accept the goals which society-at-large has already set for itself and help it attain them; he seeks to help society convert those goals so that culture becomes not necessarily what it is already seeking to be, but what faith tells the Christian that it could be, or at any rate it should be. Although this view, like the "Christ and culture in paradox" stance, affirms that man and his communities have fallen into sin and become misdirected, it also believes that the Christian and his church are here called upon, guided, and to some extent empowered by their faith to redirect and reform their society in ways which accord better with the will of God. This view is put well by Roger L. Shinn and Daniel Williams in their monograph, *We Believe,* an interpretation of the *Statement of Faith of the United Church of Christ,* which was adopted within the last decade. In commenting upon the *Statement's* assertion that Christians can rely upon God's promise to provide courage in the struggle for justice and peace, these two theologians explain:

There are two kinds of peace in Christian thinking and . . . they must not be confused. The first is a peace, an inner serenity, that comes from trust in God. It is a peace which endures in the midst of outer conflict and peril. . . . The second peace is a political peace among nations and among the people within nations. It is a peace based on justice. . . . This peace is also a gift. As Isaiah describes it, it is an eschatological peace; that is, an ultimate hope that is never realized in human history but that can influence our conduct now. At this point human efforts can make a big difference. There are policies that make for injustice and war, and policies that make for justice and peace. It is not enough that Christians pray for peace. They must work. They must enter into the "struggle for justice and peace." And their prayers will not be for some divine intervention that will suddenly end war; the prayers will be for courage and wisdom in the struggle.[19]

The same general view, although with different nuances, is set forth in the "Reconciliation in Society" section of the Confession of 1967 adopted by the United Presbyterian Church, U.S.A.:

The reconciliation of man through Jesus Christ makes it plain that enslaving poverty in a world of abundance is an intolerable violation of God's good creation. Because Jesus identified himself with the needy and the exploited, the cause of the world's poor is the cause of his disciples. . . . The church calls all men to use their abilities and possessions as gifts entrusted to them by God for the advancement of the common welfare. It encourages those forces in human society that raise men's hopes for better conditions and provide them opportunity for a decent living. A church that is indifferent to poverty, or denies responsibility in economic affairs, or is open to one social class only, or expects grati-

[19] (Philadelphia, 1966), pp. 111-12.

tude for its beneficence makes a mockery of reconciliation and can offer no acceptable worship to God.

The "transforming" view, however, provides the Christian with fewer definite guidelines to action than do the other four types. Left open are some of the following all-important questions: How dire is the specific societal situation, and how radical a transformation of it is required? What are the operational values (political, economic, etc.) of a just and loving society which will guide the Christian? How does a church organize itself to pursue the creation of that society, and what are the means "acceptable" in God's sight for that effort? How does such a church relate itself to and respond to the restraints placed upon it by other groups within the society (government, business, nonchurch groups organized for various styles of change). The "transformist" Christian and church must ask all these questions, but answers are not easy to find.

Implications for Investment. The "Christ-transforming culture" view knows that the Christian's role is not simply to "realize and conserve" existing structures and values, but to attempt to make them more consistent with those which he knows in faith. The inner logic of the position seems to require that no church resources (and certainly not its investments) should be "left out" of this work.

While these five types locate generally the various stances which Christians assume as they relate their faith to the world, they are indefinite guides to action. Although they may help churchmen discern the broad outlines of how they will want to think about a social investment program, much more will be required to give a specific focus to the difficult and complex questions which social investment decisions inevitably involve. Therefore, the remainder of the chapter will attempt to provide three other ways of viewing these problems.

PERSPECTIVE I: PURITY OR EFFECTIVENESS

To date, much of the discussion among churchmen concerning investments has focused on trying to find a way of "purifying" the church portfolios—or "winnowing" them, as one denomination has called it. By this type of initiative, the church has tried to avoid receiving income which is the "profit" derived from products or practices which it believes are immoral or "unchristian." Many churchmen now pressing for other changes in investment policy use this approach as a precedent.[20]

For some churches, especially the "Christ against culture" type, this is a consistent way of relating to society: if the church must be in contact with the wider society, that contact must be as "clean" as possible. But for most of the other stances, it is simply not a coherent position

[20] The most recent example is a social investment overture concurred in by the 1970 General Assembly of the United Presbyterian Church, U.S.A. See Appendix B.

76

unless the purification of the church will (by example, for instance) lead to a better society. In one way or another, the other four stances seek "effectiveness," not institutional purity.

There is a variety of explanations for this apparent obsession with institutional cleanliness. For some it represents both the view that stock ownership does "involve" the church with a particular corporate enterprise and the estimate that no "effective" ways exist for an investor to change socially injurious or morally repugnant corporate practice. It is true that holding stock or bonds in corporations with deleterious practices may be interpreted as implicit acquiescence to conduct that the church should not condone; but the judgment that no other effective ways exist to alter corporate practice will be challenged in chapter 4. On the other hand, some who propose the purity position doubt that those who manage the churches' investments will actually utilize the various forms of corporate persuasion available to the stockholder. This explains why those who support social investment programs have been deaf to the persistent arguments by church investment boards that it is more efficacious to "stay in and fight." Some clear indications of sincerity by church staffs and investors (such as the annual meeting appearances of church officials in response to the 1967 quarrel between Eastman Kodak and FIGHT, a Rochester community organization) could assuage church investor-dissident relations on this point.

A second and quite separable issue raised by the purity-effectiveness issue is the long-standing debate which may be labeled the "one and the many" controversy. Some church officials have contended (1) that it is not "fair" to criticize one corporation for a procedure considered objectionable without criticizing all corporations involved in the same activities; or, (2) it is unfair to censure a corporation for one practice when many of its other practices are admirable. Since these arguments often paralyze churches and make them ineffective, it is essential to examine each one carefully.

1. The first form of this argument is indeed baffling. Its strangeness becomes obvious when the argument is turned over. One assumes that a church which was especially gratified by an action or activity of a corporation of which it was part-owner would not delay commending the decision of the corporation's management until it had assured itself that it could simultaneously praise all other American corporations which had made similar decisions. The simple fact that the church holds stock in the company suggests that it has the special responsibility of making known its views about that corporation's practices. A further point here: American churches were not especially concerned that Martin Luther King, Jr., concentrated on exposing the discriminatory practices of a single municipal transportation system rather than sending letters to all the mayors of all the southern cities to request the alteration of similar existing laws. It is hard to see why the church should fail to act just because it cannot take similar action in every similar case. There is, of course, a

strong argument that treating like cases in a like manner is an important element of good moral practice; but that argument means only that the church's response should not be *capriciously different* in sanctioning (approvingly or disapprovingly) similar cases in analogous situations; it does not entail moral paralysis because of impotence to "right" (or even attempt to "right") all similar wrongs coinstantaneously.

2. Although the other form of the argument, which suggests basically that one should not condemn or commend a corporation unless all of its practice is unambiguously good or bad, is just as curious, its curiousness is more difficult to show. Corporations do and make a great variety of things. It is not, then, surprising that some of what they do will be admirable and some deleterious. But take an extreme example. If a corporation had exemplary employment practices, gave massively to the "right" causes through its charitable giving program, produced life-saving drugs at rock-bottom prices, and had installed the most modern air pollution control devices on its smoke-stacks, but caused the death or illness of thousands of children in downstream municipalities by dumping mercury into a local stream, one would probably not hesitate to condemn the corporation's water pollution practices. Why, then, have churchmen accepted the appeals of corporate executives who have asked not to be criticized in one area because they are doing well in another? Why?

Another example will suggest the answer. Although fair employment practices in a corporation's personnel department cannot negate contentions that its franchises are distributed on a discriminatory basis, they do qualify the accusation that the corporation is *entirely* racist in its practices. This qualification requires only that the allegations be precise and accurate. It does not mean that churches should refrain altogether from questioning specific offenses by corporations whose *other* activities are socially costless or are admirable. Conversely, corporations making estimable decisions deserve precise, not unqualified, commendation, but churches have not always been precise or informed in these statements, either. Meaningful and effective investment policies require the honing of tools of criticism and praise. If the church is accurate in what it does say and makes an effort to see the whole, not just the part, it need not suffer from moral paralysis, even though it must often act without complete knowledge of all of a corporation's activities.

PERSPECTIVE II: APPLICATION OF CHURCH POLICIES TO INVESTMENT

Since the church cannot know everything about every aspect of the American corporation, the question arises: Where can a church look to delimit its range of social investment concerns? The best sources are the policy statements (the resolutions accepted by church annual meetings; the authorization of programs, priorities, etc.). The General Synod of the United Church of Christ did this when it created its Committee on Financial Investments to draw up a social investment policy. It instructed the Committee to "establish criteria and make recommendations toward substantial use of investments . . . to promote maximum social impact *based on established* General Synod policies." [21]

The Committee report, recently adopted by that church's executive council, took these instructions seriously. The first part of its document studies the evolution of the church's social policy and the implications of those policies for investments. It pulls together the basic themes, concerns and principles of the church so that investors can deal with new issues by employing this section to determine whether and how the church should respond to or initiate action as an investor. Besides giving specificity to the church's basic "view" of culture for the use of investors, this approach has many ancillary benefits. It keeps church program and church investment efforts from working at cross-purposes, and it provides an extra incentive for examining carefully church "program budgets" to make certain that their focus is consistent with the direction of the church's proclaimed mission and related programs.

PERSPECTIVE III: SUBSTANTIVE CHRISTIAN ETHICS

Obviously, an increasingly complex and confused social situation requires clearheaded thinking about the relation

[21] Italics added. *Minutes,* Seventh General Synod, 1969, p. 71.

of faith to actual practice. Not only the church's heart, but its mind must be in the right place if it is to play any moral leadership role in society. In recent years Christian ethicists have debated, not only methodological questions, but substantive social issues as well. Their thinking, however, has not often informed the church's policy on issues which ethical debate could help clarify. The Vietnam War question, a source of contention in the churches as well as in the society generally, is an example.

Christians have responded to the war in many ways and implicitly employed many ethical categories, such as "just war" ones.[22] These categories have sometimes provided ethicists with a way of separating the issues in order to arrive at more precise and consistent judgments.[23] Some Christians feel the Christian has the responsibility to render judgments about the justness of a war's cause, its means, its intention, as well as the reasonable hope of its success, its proportionality, and the authority of its prosecutors. For others, no war is acceptable. For still others, the citizen can only judge the justness of the means employed.[24] As the debate over the role of the military in Southeast Asia continues and the debate over the role of the priorities on military spending heats up, the need for precision in church investment policies will

[22] See Ralph B. Potter, *War and Moral Discourse* (Richmond, Va., 1969).

[23] The word "sometimes" needs emphasis; just war categories are more helpful in raising the right questions than in providing the answers.

[24] It is possible to correlate these various views, at least partially, with some of Niebuhr's five types.

grow. It is possible that by clarifying complex questions, the churches can agree on some issues which have caused dissension in the past, assuming, of course, that a church's basic theological affirmations and the ethics derived from them guide their actions. For example, most churches probably oppose indiscriminate killing of noncombatants; and yet, it is now being argued, various kinds of modern weapons systems make such distinctions impossible.[25] If the issues can remain in focus, agreement on some social investment initiatives may be significant. On other issues church memberships may disagree: for example, on efforts to persuade major defense producers not to accept military contracts. The significant thing here is that the points of commonality and diversity should be determined by intelligent marshaling of evidence and informed use of the theological and ethical categories which serve as the church's inner logic. It might be good both for Christian ethicists and for the churches if they rediscovered each other in this type of endeavor.[26]

In summary, this chapter avers that, when viewed

[25] The criticism by opponents of the war (Honeywell, producer of anti-personnel weapons, and Dow Chemical, former producer of napalm), is often generated by concern that the weapons these companies produce kill indiscriminately.

[26] One large "para-religious" organization is now attempting to establish a bank of information on the practices of U.S. corporations in regard to conservation, pollution, corporate giving to education, and negotiation procedures with foreign governments on foreign trade arrangements. But it is also considering a proposal that, along with its information, it furnish a variety of ethical perspectives on these problems—thus providing institutions with both facts and the value options through which to interpret them.

financially, the churches are part of the genus of institutions known as the private nonprofit sector. It argues that this group of institutions has special social responsibilities when it invests. Churches, moreover, are a species of that genus and important differences, as well as points of similarity, are found among them. H. Richard Niebuhr's five views of the relationship between faith and culture explain generally why that diversity exists. The three perspectives just discussed offer a further way of helping the churches to think through and find real points of commonality and diversity among themselves.

II
MEANINGFUL SOCIAL INVEST-
MENT INITIATIVES FROM THE
CHURCHES: AN OUTLINE OF
POSSIBILITIES AND LIMITATIONS

Unfortunately, much confusion and, in some cases, hostility, caused in large part by inadequate or incomplete information, has accompanied virtually every stage of the development of social investment initiatives in the churches. Systematic examination of what a stockholder can and cannot do and under what conditions he can do it will not altogether remove this confusion and anxiety. Clarification of the complex issues involved may help resolve disputes, however. Adoption of a meaningful social investment policy will doubtless mean that those who have become competent in investing with a single goal

in mind—increasing the funds available for church programs—will have to develop new competencies and ways
of handling funds, and discover new perspectives on their
work. It will almost certainly require accepting persons
with previously unrequired skills and talents into the investment decision-making processes.

The two chapters of this section (chapters 3 and 4)
outline the options available to the investor who seeks
concrete ways of manifesting his social concern. Some of
these options are available for investing any funds held
by churches; others apply only to funds whose investment is limited or "restricted" in very general ways only.
Elucidation of the types of legal and institutional restraints
upon the investment of different kinds of church funds
will suggest how those restraints actually apply to the
utilization of the "options" described here and will be dealt
with later, in chapters 5 and 6.

Even for the experienced investor (let alone those un-
initiated in the law and in finance), this section will be
complicated new terrain, because a whole range of data
is brought together in uncommon ways. The author does
not claim to have mastered it, but the parameters are
staked out here, and many of the key signposts indicated.
The fainthearted and those ideologically committed, either
to standing pat or to ignoring important distinctions and
restrictions, will not enjoy the ride. Nevertheless, the
future of a viable and living church, guided and sustained
by an inner *raison d'être,* may depend upon just such
intricate and perplexing journeys as this one.

3

The Corporate Investment Element: Powers and Limitations of the Institutional Investor

An investor can attempt to alter or encourage a corporation's practice in four basic ways: (1) through his decisions to buy or sell stock and other securities; (2) through his employment of the investor's proxy prerogatives available to owners of voting stock; (3) through litigation against the corporation where common stock is held; and (4) through various forms of informal persuasion. What follows is an extended discussion of each of these options.

BUYING AND SELLING STOCKS

The three different options possible here may be treated together. These are the options most people think of when responsible investment policies are proposed. The first two options have been called "negative sanctions;" the third is sometimes called "incentive" investment.

(a) a decision to *sell* stock in protest over practices or products deemed to be especially deleterious;

(b) a decision *not to buy* stocks in such companies until particular practices are discontinued or initiated;

(c) a decision to look with special favor upon the stock of corporations whose general practices are deemed to be socially beneficial.

Two separate arguments have been made for exercising these options: first, that the investor can purify his portfolio, either by removing the taint from it or by supporting the beneficial practices of specific corporations; second, that such actions can change corporate practices.

The first of these arguments is self-evidently true and needs no buttressing. If a church's self-understanding requires that it cannot be involved with institutions whose activities it does not condone, then it should follow one or all of these buy-sell options. The problem is not with the rationale, but with the implementation. As long as the nonpurchase of stocks of alcohol or tobacco producers was the whole of a social investment policy, there was no problem. However, an example will show why these simpler days appear to be gone.

In the continuing controversy over corporations maintaining plants and sales relationships with South Africa, many churches have considered "sell and no purchase" policies in about 275 of such corporations. Some churchmen argue that many of these corporations are among (1) the most financially sound, and (2) socially progressive as regards domestic policies in the country (Xerox and IBM are often cited as examples here). Still, as long as a church is concerned only about this specific issue, it could, even without crippling financial loss to itself, develop a "clean" portfolio by selling and not purchasing securities in these corporations.

But add concern about armament production to the issues which disturb the church in search of a clean portfolio, and things become more difficult. Does one defense contract defile a company? If so, then the social investors' "no-purchase list" gets very long indeed. Some suggest that the top 100 defense producers are most culpable, but the church seeking purity finds it hard to see why. Further, this list is itself deceptive. The lives of some smaller companies depend heavily upon defense contracts, and hence the percentage of their defense businesses is very high, even though they are not in the top 100. It appears that the church seeking a clean portfolio has to decide either (1) to avoid investment in corporations with any defense contracts, or (2) to develop a moral understanding which specifies which defense products are unacceptable. At any rate, the investor concerned to purify his portfolio by avoiding investment in corporations doing business with South Africa or the Pentagon, will have very significantly reduced his investment options.

Now add the issues of (1) pollution, (2) fair employment practices, (3) wage standards in foreign countries, etc., etc., each of which involves problems similar to those already discussed, and the clean portfolio becomes an almost impossible ideal. The point is not that criteria cannot be developed for cleaner portfolios; but that relative ethics are often unacceptable for the church in search of purity. The object is normally "clean," not "cleaner" portfolios. Hence, one likely result of efforts to find untainted portfolios will be the collapse of social investment initiatives altogether. The search for purity, a concept which tends to be absolutist, often leads to moral paralysis in today's complex world.

Those churches which buy or sell specified stocks, hoping to influence the corporation, will want to look at a very different range of questions. Is it the case—and if so, precisely how—that the sale or purchase of stock affects a corporation? This question has led to two basic responses: (1) that sale or purchase itself will affect the corporation *economically* and hence induce management to change a particular practice; or (2) that the symbolic action of selling or purchasing will have a "public" effect and *indirectly* influence the desired result. These two proposals deserve separate consideration.

The Corporate Investment Element

1. An economics study done recently at Yale University tested the contention that the economic effects of stock purchase or sale would induce a desired change in management policy. The researchers looked at several recent cases in which large blocks of stock in a corporation were sold for what were known to be noneconomic reasons. In none of these cases did the price of the stock weaken significantly, or stock values remain even slightly depressed for more than one day. In the most celebrated case, the Ford Foundation decided to sell a large block of its Ford Motor Company stock. In one transaction which involved five percent of the outstanding shares of Ford stock, prices slipped only slightly in the morning of the day they were traded. In fact, however, very few institutions own anything approaching five percent of a corporation's stock; for example, an institution with an endowment approaching a half-billion dollars often owns less than one percent of the stock of most corporations in which it invests.[1]

What would have been the effect upon management if the effect on market price had been stronger? Corporate stock prices are important to corporate managements in only a few ways. For example, they reflect confidence (or lack of it) in existing management and hence, over the long run, could affect shareholder decisions concerning the retention of existing management. Secondly, they affect the ability of a corporation to secure new funds for capitalization (that is, to underwrite new expansion pro-

[1] I am indebted here to the work of Morton Kahn and Bard Potter, participants in a course entitled, "Yale's Investments," Yale University, 1969-70.

grams). Again, if it was known that noneconomic factors had caused temporary stock value depression, these two considerations would not have great importance. The holdings of the investing institution, however, *are* affected. If a social investor were to succeed in driving stock prices down, his own stock sales would be the ones most immediately affected—he would sustain the loss. He would also be paying added brokerage fees. Any effectiveness argument involves some sort of calculus of costs and benefits. In the case of the *economic* argument for protesting *sale* of stock, the benefits seem to be miniscule and the costs quite high.

Several arguments counter this analysis. First, it refers only to the protest sale and not to the incentive purchase of corporate stocks. In some instances the purchase of a stock in a small and especially progressive public corporation might help it significantly in sustaining its stock price. This would be even truer if the transaction involved a new issue or a corporate bond, since success in selling these securities would affect the company's ability to expand. This point is important, but cases in which it would be relevant are rare.[2]

A second argument is that while a single institution's investments could not affect prices significantly, concerted institutional initiatives could be a powerful force in the market.[3] While this is probably true, it should be

[2] A more effective type of incentive investment will be discussed under the "creative" investments heading in the next chapter.

[3] See William L. Cary, *Cases and Materials on Corporations* (New York, 1969), p. 235 for an analysis of the percentage of the holdings of various institutions on the NYSE in 1968.

noted that a possible deterrent to the effort to "organize" institutions for an effective protest sale is anti-trust legislation which limits the ways in which efforts to coordinate concerted institutional action may be carried out.[4]

In sum, in rare cases the economic effect of buying or selling stock may have a beneficial social impact, but in virtually no cases could a policy decision not to buy a stock have an impact.

2. Those who argue the case for sale or purchase for effect rarely have in mind only the economic impact. They often consider more important the symbolic effect of one

[4] Both the rationale behind this legislation and the nature of its applicability to shareholders in pursuit of a social goal through the selling of stock are very complex matters. Adequate explanation cannot be set forth here, but the theory is not difficult to sketch. Antitrust legislation and procedure in this area have been developed to protect individual corporations from conspiracy-like efforts by persons or groups acting in concert to subvert a competitor. In an article "Cooperation among Competitors" (61 *Northwestern Law Review,* 865, 871) Donald Turner, former Chief of the Anti-Trust Division of the Justice Department, has said: "It is one thing for competitors to voluntarily impose upon themselves some limitations on competition. . . . It is quite another to use collective economic pressures to drive third parties out of business which are perfectly lawful and lawfully conducted, or to coerce third parties into abandoning economic decisions which no law forbids them from making."

The key issue in such cases, however, is whether or not there is an actual series of "coincidences" which imply agreement to sell or boycott a stock. If a large group of investors, acting individually, sold their stocks at the same time, such an implication might well be drawn. It is only such simultaneous action, however, which is likely to have even the short-term effect of driving the market price down. (I am indebted to the work of Olaf Hellen, participant in the course, "Yale's Investments," Yale University, 1969-70, for some of the information used in this footnote.)

or more large institutions which do not buy stock of a particular corporation or sell specific stock in protest. An important test of this option was made between 1967 and 1969. A number of churches, other organizations and individuals severed their financial relationships with U.S. banks which had been maintaining a revolving credit agreement with the South African government.

Public concern grew. By fall, 1969, several more church boards had decided to sever banking relationships with these institutions. During the course of the three-year effort, several high bank officials reportedly told churchmen that the campaign had very importantly affected the banks' "public image." On November 15, 1969, the South African government made public its decision not to seek the biennial extension of the loan arrangement when it came up for review the following January, 1970, saying that it no longer needed the credit arrangement. This explanation contradicts many analyses of the economic situation in South Africa at the time. A report that the South African government had been seeking new credit arrangements in Europe the preceding summer does, if true, further undermine the rationale offered. The question is, did the churches' efforts cause the banks to ask South Africa not to request continuance of the credit arrangement? If so, protest sale or withdrawal, when combined with effective publication of such decisions and extended discussions with management, etc., may be an effective form of corporate persuasion.

Several qualifications must be made, however. As noted

before, sale of securities is a relatively blunt approach. The act itself of withdrawing from involvement in the company does not symbolically represent the precise issue which is raised. If the action were taken against a corporation whose primary business involvement was in South Africa,[5] this would not matter. But in the case of the New York banks, the involvement was, relatively speaking, not extensive. The banks enumerated the "good" things they were doing[6] in addition to defending their operations in South Africa. The issues became fuzzy, at least for those who heard the arguments pro and con secondhand.

The argument that divestment (sale of stock) or a decision to sell in protest is a blunt tool which is not the most effective means is persuasive, however, only if other approaches to the corporation are shown to be more effective. To test that hypothesis, the other three corporate investment "options" must be examined.

USE OF THE CORPORATE PROXY

A more general social policy question must be addressed before individual analysis of this or the two remaining options makes good sense. Chapter 1 commented upon the growing separation of the stockholder (the owner) from the management in most corporations which has developed in this economy. We have also seen that the

[5] Several mining and manufacturing companies are examples here.
[6] An irrelevant point, as suggested in chapter 2, but persuasive to some, nevertheless.

1934 Securities Exchange Act attempted to alter that state of affairs by providing conditions conducive to "corporate democracy"—that is, more actual involvement by owners in corporate decisions. This congressional intention has not been realized. Only when a corporation has gotten itself into very troubled economic straits, have stockholders mobilized to exercise their options to remove or reinstruct management. The manager has, therefore, become relatively autonomous and, while he operates among conflicting pressures, the only pressure normally applied by the stockholder is the implicit one which spurs him *either* to do well enough to pay high dividends *or* to maintain a rate of growth high enough to keep stock prices going up (and hence provide the shareholder with capital gains based upon high dividends expected at a later date).

Many have argued that the "autonomy" of the manager is good, or at least preferable, to increased stockholder involvement in the corporation's life. These arguments include the following: (1) the shareholder is normally a speculator who has no abiding interest in the corporation and hence is more akin to a consumer looking for a good product than he is to an owner who will care for his property; (2) it is precisely the autonomy of the manager which has allowed him to support the long-range self-interest of the corporation and/or its initiatives toward social responsibility; increased stockholder activity may stifle these efforts; (3) if anyone should have a greater say, it is the workers, the laborers, and others most directly affected by corporate activities—the investor is the least affected of the corporate constituencies.[7] Those who make these arguments see the concept of shareholder democracy as a "legal fiction" (since it is so rarely employed) and are not sorry for this. The author disagrees. At this time —or at least until the spring of 1969—shareholder democracy is a "legal fiction" as regards the conduct of corporate affairs. But it is one of the only "legalities" through which a wider public can still directly influence the massive centers of corporate power which now exist. In a recent decision by the United States Court of Appeals (which we will have occasion to study at greater length), the opinion written by Justice Tamm argues against "management's patently illegitimate claim of power to treat modern corporations with their vast resources as personal satrapies implementing personal, political, or moral predilections." [8] The point is clear: sources of countervailing power must be found to keep American society open until and unless some other way of distributing power is found. The correlate of this is that while "stockholders" do not represent all the people—and perhaps not those most affected by the corporation, they do represent *more* of it than does any single group of corporate execu-

[7] Arguments such as these may be found in Abram Chayes, "The Modern Corporation and the Rule of Law"; *The Corporation in Modern Society,* ed. Edward Mason; and J.A.C. Hetherington, "Fact and Legal Theory: Shareholders, Managers, and Corporate Responsibility," *Stanford Law Review,* January, 1969.

[8] *Medical Committee for Human Rights* v. *Securities Exchange Commission,* United States Court of Appeals, for the District of Columbia Circuit, July 8, 1970.

tives or directors. Corporate law avers that most corporations exist for the benefit of the stockholder.

A primary hope of this book is that stockholders represent a broad enough cross section of the society and will care enough about exercising their legal prerogatives as owners of corporate America to insist on corporate practices which will work toward a more just and equitable society. Even the "Christ of culture" Christians cannot argue that things are going so well now that increased stockholder involvement will throw a wrench into a well-oiled machine whose output is unqualifiedly good for the commonweal. In discussing his support of Campaign GM, one prominent economist recently said, "General Motors management needs some fresh air." While stockholder prerogatives are not the only way to get that fresh air to the corporation (government and labor still have their roles) and while some younger members of management are now bringing it in with them, the stockholder can still play an important role.

A discussion between a top steel corporation executive and a young professor is relevant here. The professor, who held a tiny block of a steel producer's stock, wrote the president of the company a stiff protest note concerning several specific aspects of his corporation's activities. The president sent one of his assistants to discuss the letter, and after a two-hour talk, the executive remarked: "Many of us in corporate management are saying the same things you are. It's an uphill struggle with the old-liners. Only pressure such as persons like you are bring-

ing will allow us to do what you have been talking about."
Although corporate democracy is no platform upon which
to build a political program, it may be an important element in reform.

What can a shareholder of common stock do if he is to
use his prerogatives? [9] Most obviously, he can exercise his
voting rights—or initiate proxy contests himself. Until
July 8, 1970, this option was severely limited in its scope.
A stockholder could always try to persuade other stockholders to attend the annual meeting and raise the question of management practice there, but the difficulties of
doing this successfully were overwhelming. We will only
allude to several of them here: it is impossible to get
any sizable number of shareholders of a national corporation to an annual meeting; the difficulties of obtaining a
shareholder list are monumental; and the possibility of
the chairman ruling a social investing proposal out-of-
order is very great.[10]

[9] This discussion will be limited to voting stock. There are, of
course, many other kinds of securities, but the rights of ownership
do not accrue to those holding these other securities. An example
is the publicly traded corporate bond. The same set of factors involved
in socially motivated purchase or sale apply to these holdings as to
common shares. In other words, the bondholder has little financial
impact. Since he is not an owner, but a lender (and often an *indirect* lender), the avenues of expression discussed below are less
open to him. Little or no work has been done on whether investors
holding securities other than common stock can realistically hope to
influence corporate managers.

[10] The 1969 annual meetings of Commonwealth Edison of Chicago
and Honeywell of Minneapolis are cases in point. Apparently, however, the Commonwealth Edison campaign was successful in per-

Another option is one where shareholders withhold their proxies from management and publicize their reasons for doing so. This action is similar to protest sale of stock, except that the annual meeting could serve as the platform for a statement of the issue. It may also be more persuasive if a large number withhold their proxies since the socially concerned remain shareholders and may, therefore, express their views at shareholder meetings. Some Eastman-Kodak shareholders did this in 1967 when they opposed the way management had dealt with FIGHT, a largely black community organization in Kodak's home office city of Rochester, New York. Kodak had repudiated an agreement made by a management official with the organization. FIGHT bought ten shares of Kodak stock, sent hundreds of letters to churches and concerned individuals, asking them to withhold their proxies from management, and succeeded in persuading investors holding 34,000 shares to do so. Howard Spragg, of the Board FOR Homeland Ministries of the United Church of Christ and other church officials, holding over 11,000 of these proxies, questioned management's action in this case on the floor of the meeting. A great deal of national attention was focused on this situation and the events leading up to it. Although cause-and-effect relationships are difficult to specify, Kodak and FIGHT reached agreement on the chief issue of job training soon after the meeting.

---

suading management to alter some of its pollution policies, and instrumental in convincing the Chicago City Council of the need for an ordinance requiring utilities to burn fuels with lower sulphur content.

Whether such approaches, which do not involve any actual voting of the proxies for a resolution proposed by a socially conscious investor, would be effective in other than exceptional cases is debatable, however.

Why not have the stockholders vote on the question at issue? The answer to this question is complex, and at the time of writing, unclear. To put the matter much too simply, a stockholder may request that the management place a resolution with a supporting statement of not more than 100 words [11] on the proxy statement which it sends out and upon which all shareholders may vote. Management may refuse only if the proposal (a) violates the rules and regulations developed by the Securities Exchange Commission "for the protection of the investor" in accord with Section 14 of the Securities Exchange Act of 1934; (b) does not accord with the law of the state in which the company is incorporated; and/or (c) relates to the conduct of the ordinary business of the corporation.[12]

In deciding what constitutes the protection of the investor, however, the SEC in Rule 14a-8 (c) (2) had determined that management could exclude a proposal in which it "clearly" appears that the proposal is submitted "primarily for the purpose of promoting general economic, political, racial, religious, social or similar views." The SEC has argued that it adopted this rule in order to protect the investor from being pestered by proxy proposals

[11] The management rebuttal statement has no word limit.
[12] I have been aided in this section by the work of law student Richard W. Cass, participant in the course, "Yale's Investments," Yale University, 1969-70.

which, in advancing a special cause of the investor, were irrelevant to the welfare of the corporation. While the SEC had for some time excluded proposals of this general character, it did not develop the phraseology just quoted until after a 1951 case (*Greyhound* v. *Peck*) involving an effort to force Greyhound to integrate seating in its buses in the South. The General Motors management refused to include the nine resolutions proposed by Campaign GM (later the Project on Corporate Responsibility) partly on the basis of this ruling. The SEC supported General Motors' decision on seven of them.[18]

However, a recent and far-reaching decision by Justice Tamm of the United States Court of Appeals (District of Columbia Circuit), on which the other two members of the panel concurred, has ordered the SEC to alter its rules. Generally, the issue at stake was whether the Dow Chemical Company had to include a shareholder resolution by the Medical Committee for Human Rights, proposing that the company stop producing napalm unless Dow could ensure that the product would not be used against human beings. Of import here is the general issue of stockholder rights, not the specific issue. Dow refused to place the resolution on its proxy statement, the SEC upheld

---

[18] The proposals accepted advocated (1) the creation of a shareholders committee for social responsibility with a specific mandate to examine a wide range of GM policies and report to stockholders by March, 1971; and (2) the addition of three new directors to the board (for the purpose of adding representatives of the public to the Board, although this was specified in the "supporting statement," not the resolution).

the management's decision, and the Medical Committee took the SEC ruling to court.

The decision stressed the following point:[14]

No reason has been advanced in the present proceeding which leads to the conclusion that management may properly place obstacles in the path of shareholders who wish to present to their co-owners in accord with applicable state law, the question of whether they wish to have their assets used in a manner which they believe to be more socially responsible but possibly less profitable than that which is dictated by present company policy.

Profit was not a relevant factor in the case, since Dow claimed that it had *lost* money on the contract. The court also questioned "whether the corporate proxy rules can be employed as a shield to isolate such managerial decisions from shareholder control," and called "implausible" the idea that the existing SEC rules "could be harmonized with the philosophy of corporate democracy which Congress embodied in Section 14(a) of the Securities Exchange Act of 1934." The court did not question that proposals delimiting "management's legitimate need for freedom to apply its expertise in matters of day-to-day business judgment" would fall outside the bounds of stockholder prerogatives, nor did it criticize the SEC's ruling

[14] To obtain a copy, write the Clerk of the Court, the United States Court of Appeals, the District of Columbia Circuit, Washington, D.C. and enclose one dollar. The case is *Medical Committee for Human Rights* v. *Securities Exchange Commission,* decided July 8, 1970. The case number is 23,105.

that proxy statements should not bring to the shareholder's attention issues of a *general* moral or social character not involving the corporation's activities. But it argued that, where moral and social issues are directly related to a corporation's practice, the solicitation of shareholder views is entirely appropriate.

The story of what all this means and where it all leads is still to be told. Except in the unlikely event that it appeals the case to the Supreme Court, the SEC will have to alter its 14a-8 (c) (2) rule in a way which means that the concerned social investor will (1) have more social issues raised for him on proxy statements and (2) have the opportunity to raise issues himself. Hence the stockholder will be able to specify those aspects of corporate activities which he considers deleterious and have them raised without resorting to the less discriminating method of selling stocks of corporations only one part of whose practice or policy he finds objectionable. It probably also means that affirmative stockholder resolutions, encouraging corporations to undertake new initiatives of a socially responsible sort, can be included.

General Motors stockholders were asked to vote on this second type of proposal in the spring of 1969. But that only raises a further question: Won't management always win? If the result of the GM vote is taken as a bellwether, then the answer must surely be "yes." Despite good publicity and a relatively sophisticated campaign, the Project G. M. proposals each received less than three percent of the proxies.[15] But this result must be put into perspective in several ways.

To start with, it was the first serious proxy campaign of its type. For many persons, the issue raised basic investment policy questions for both institutional and individual investors which could not be resolved in the several months prior to this annual meeting. Secondly, because it did not involve a specific moral or social issue relating to the corporation's practice,[16] a great many "philosophical" questions about how businesses should be run were raised in the discussion.[17] In a number of cases, hesitancy about the ambiguity of the proposals led to abstention on or rejection of the proposals. In other words, the specific proposals, not the idea of social investment, may have caused the defeat. Thirdly, the campaign did have an effect. Reports from several sources indicate that, as a result of the campaign, the GM management has seriously taken up many of the issues. There is already a concrete manifestation of that. General Motors recently announced the formation of a committee of five members (none of whom is an officer) to have special responsibilities

[15] Management has a decided advantage in these contests. Unless a shareholder indicates that he is abstaining on a particular issue, his vote is often accorded as management directs (Rule 14a-4 (b)). Management picks up many votes in this way, since shareholder inertia is very great, and many proxies are returned unmarked.

[16] It involved only the question of whether the board should be expanded to include three new board members who would bring new perspectives to the board and a shareholder committee to monitor the corporation's performance and report to the shareholders.

[17] Not that they should not be raised, of course. The point is that they will be difficult to resolve.

in matters that relate to public policy. While its membership is definitely not what the Project would have chosen, it does indicate increasing management sensitivity to the type of issues raised during the spring of 1970.

In sum, the combination of the Court of Appeals decision and the General Motors campaign and similar campaigns have opened a new avenue for the investor who wants to bring informed and well-articulated social issues to the attention of management and fellow stockholders in a forceful way. The question, of course, is whether the churches will take the lead in ensuring that this new option is used responsibly and for the purposes which it seeks. Any such new possibility can be effectively ruined if it is used capriciously or poorly. If stockholders begin to receive proxy statements with long lists of ill-informed proposals, the shareholder will likely throw them away or vote automatically with management. This new option is tailored to the social investment purposes and needs of many churches and churchmen. Will they use that option well? [18]

SHAREHOLDER LITIGATION

Under the new ruling the proxy possibility can be a relatively inexpensive one. On the other hand, litigation

[18] I am indebted to Richard W. Cass, participant in the "Yale's Investments" course, Yale University, 1969-70, for some of the research which informed this section. However, many important legal points have not received adequate treatment here. William L. Cary's *Cases and Materials on Corporations*, New York, 1969, pp. 229-361, should be consulted for a more extended discussion.

will be costly. Furthermore, there will be fewer instances in which it is a "live" option. Corporate law allows the stockholder legal recourse, however, if he believes that management's practices are *ultra vires* (that is, beyond the powers granted by the state charter), negligent, illegal, fraudulent or involve a clear abuse of discretion. To be successful in the state court, however, he must show that, as a result of management's very poor business judgment, he and his fellow stockholders will sustain a financial loss; or that a management decision involves the corporation in illegal activity for which it may be prosecuted unless it alters the practice. Through such legal action, called a "derivative suit," the stockholder takes management to court on behalf of the other stockholders in the company. The following example shows where it might apply to the social investor. A company, operating in violation of state pollution laws, has not yet been prosecuted by the public authorities. The stockholder can bring a derivative suit in order to force the management to comply with the pollution law. Again in this case, the initiative, and not its ultimate success in court, could bring the desired result, since the action might persuade management to comply in order to avoid prosecution or harmful publicity, or might cause the public authority to take action to force compliance.

The impediments to successful derivative suits are truly monumental. For example, in some cases (though dependent upon relevant state law), if the shareholder holds less than five percent of the outstanding stock of the corporation or his stock has a market value of less than $50,-000, he must post security to cover the "reasonable" legal and other costs incurred by the company in its legal defense;[19] if the stockholder loses, he forfeits the security. Of course, the litigant's own legal expenses in the drawn-out legal processes common in this type of suit will be substantial. The investor should also be advised that success rates in this sort of suit are low.

The social investor would use this avenue only rarely. If it was deemed to be the most effective way of pursuing a church social policy in extreme cases of corporate abuse and public authority recalcitrance, however, it might well be justified.

CORPORATE PERSUASION

As noted earlier, the most common argument against the protest sale of stock is that the church can be more effective by "staying in." Part of what "staying in" may involve is informed management persuasion. While those most agitated about an issue normally do not consider this a serious argument, they often overlook its potential. Partly because it is a stockholder and partly because of the persons and ideals it represents, the church can undertake various forms of corporate persuasion. This may be

[19] The rationale for this stringent requirement is to ascertain that there is at least a presumption that the stockholder is sufficiently interested in the company, in that his legal action is likely to have been motivated by a concern for the corporation's welfare and not for personal gain.

an especially efficacious route in those cases where the aim is to persuade corporations to make new social initiatives rather than to criticize existing practices. The "autonomy" of management begins to cut the other way here. If the analysis in chapter 1 and Appendix A is correct, business executives are facing a crisis of legitimacy and may be receptive to some proposals concerning its social responsibilities. Efforts through letters or, better, through personal discussions prior to public pronouncements or more "formal" initiatives may allow management to hear the church's case before the corporation is pushed into a public posture of opposition. Several such church initiatives *have* been successful. Even if unsuccessful, the informal persuasion approach may lay the best groundwork for the more "public" initiatives.

Persuasion need not always be "quiet," however. When delegates to the 1967 General Synod of the United Church of Christ discovered indications of discriminatory employment policies in the Cincinnati hotels in which the Synod was convening, discussion between local management and a church committee resulted in a phone call to the national headquarters, the immediate response of a company vice-president, conferences with local community leaders about the situation, and a later visit to the hotels by the executive vice-president to determine the progress which had been made in altering personnel policies. While this example does not involve the church as an investor, analogies to the investor role can easily be drawn. Man-

agement persuasion by the company's "part owners" is an
option which has always been open to the investor, but
one which has only recently been used effectively by
churches. It is normally an important "first step" and
may on some occasions turn out to be the only one needed.

In summary of this chapter, the four options discussed
here should demonstrate that, in Adolph Berle's terms,
the investor is "passive and receptive" only if he chooses
to be. Business is increasingly conscious of its image as a
corporate citizen, and, as this sensitivity grows, the possibilities will increase for the church to effect in the nation's marketplace the operative values and practices it
espouses. But the church must *act* on those Christian
values which it proclaims from the pulpit. The transfer
of what is expressed there to what is practiced in daily
life is difficult; but that is only another reason why the
church needs to preach its gospel, where people try to live
it out. The church cannot be so ill-informed about what
really happens in daily life that laymen can say, as one
has: "If I took the advice of the clergy, I would either
be out of business in a month or involved in twice as
many moral perplexities as I started with."[20] Perhaps
when the church begins to act in those places where it
already is—as an investor—to connect its own "inner
logic" with its own activities and to influence others, the
lack of effective communication, which the statement just

[20] Clarence C. Walton, *Ethos and the Executive* (Englewood Cliffs,
N.J., 1969), p. 51.

quoted demonstrates, will be overcome. That does not mean timidity or fear of stepping on toes, for the real church and marketplace dialogue will best take place in encounters where the church is forthright about its message and its relevance to daily life.

4
The Creative Investment Element: Going the Extra Mile in Investment

Social investment may involve the church not only in being the management's keeper but also in seeking out and supporting the efforts of those who have been essentially by-passed in the existing economic cycle. The churches and the foundations have long engaged in grant-giving efforts to the poor, the inadequately-housed, and the sick. Surely the church will and should continue in these efforts. Indeed the church seems to be increasing its support of these causes. The United Presbyterian Church's "Fund for the Self-Development of People," adopted by the 1970 General Assembly, and the United Church of

Christ's continuing "Crisis in the Nation" appeal begun in 1969 are examples. Social investment policy is distinct from the grant or program processes, however. Investment funds are not grant funds, although they do provide the base from which program efforts derive the additional "yield" for their support.

In the previous section the discussion focused on funds invested in corporations from which such a yield was expected. In this section will be discussed the various opportunities available for placing those investment monies so that the principal itself will be working for the social impact that the churches seek even as they produce yield for their other programs.[1] Some of the many reasons why all of the churches' monies are not invested in this way will be discussed in the next chapter.

A "creative investment" always involves placing funds in projects with one of the following characteristics: (1) projects or enterprises which do not normally attract the attention of the average investor, although they could provide yield and security equivalent to those enterprises in which funds are usually invested; (2) projects which protect the principal but do not produce as high a return or yield as usual investments do; (3) projects which have a high return potential but involve a risk to the principal; and (4) placement in projects, which involves both a risk of principal and lower projected return. It is important

[1] This area is now "exploding" and insurance firms, banks, and corporations, as well as nonprofit institutions are getting involved in it.

113

first to clarify each of these categories before examining other issues which "creative investment" raises.

INVESTMENTS WHICH INVOLVE GOING OUTSIDE NORMAL CHANNELS TO ACHIEVE THE SAME RESULTS

Most church investors retain a variety of deposit accounts in banks. These accounts vary in size from time to time, depending on the availability of other investment opportunities. Investors maintain them in order to be able to take advantage of new investment opportunities as they occur and receive banking services at lower cost. In addition, most investors simply desire to maintain a cash reserve. Some of these deposit arrangements are equivalent to the simple savings account; some are certificates of deposit arrangements. Traditionally, the church investor has maintained these deposits in mainline banks. However, a number of churches, foundations, and corporations have recently been making these deposits in "minority-owned banks." The Federal Deposit Insurance Corporation and other government insurance programs guarantee most of these kinds of accounts for up to $20,000, which means that the principal is extraordinarily secure and that the investor receives the going rate for this type of account (normally four and a half to six percent). As far as the author knows, those churches which have followed this "creative" investment option have limited their deposits to the guaranteed amount. The Board of World Ministries of the United Church of Christ, for example, has such limited deposits in seven minority-controlled banks. Many corporations have not been so cautious, however. Olin and Glen Alden, for example, have deposits in excess of $1 million in such banks, and a number of others have deposits of hundreds of thousands of dollars.[2]

Several social benefits accrue from such an investment. Not only do they help support minority-owned ventures, but they also make available additional loan funds to minority people often inadequately served by other banks.

While it is not, strictly speaking, an investment, a similar activity supports black-owned or managed investment firms when such firms are chosen as the institutional investor's broker. This procedure is analogous, then, to the church's efforts to buy from minority suppliers, realtors, etc.

LOW-RISK, BUT POTENTIALLY LOWER-RETURN INVESTMENTS

In cooperation with a variety of government programs, the church can provide important seed money (initial capital, the remainder of which is obtained from banks or insurance companies) for social impact areas of the econ-

[2] See Michael Brower and Doyle Little, "White Help for Black Business," *Harvard Business Review,* May-June, 1970, p. 12.

omy by making loans, for example, to nonprofit, low-income housing sponsors. (Some of these may be local churches or regional church bodies.) If the project is launched, these loans are fully recuperable out of FHA-guaranteed funds;[3] interest may be low or be at going commercial rates. In such cases, the social benefit is that the interest rate for the sponsor during the construction period is less, and the ultimate cost to the tenant or future owner is thus lower.

HIGHER-RISK, BUT POTENTIALLY HIGH-RETURN INVESTMENTS

The development of many programs aiding the minority businessman continues. The Commerce Department has recently authorized the development of local MESBIC's (Minority Enterprise Small Business Investment Corporations) modeled after similar corporations formed in accord with the Small Business Investment Companies Act of 1958 (SBIC), but allowing for higher-risk loans than the normal SBIC's. An investment of $150,000 to establish a MESBIC could attract $300,000 in government funds and would provide the base for additional bank loans, ninety percent of which the Small Business Administration would guarantee. The result is that $150,-

---

[3] Government regulations in this area are, however, constantly changing, and efforts to ascertain current ones should be made.

000 initial capital in MESBIC can generate two and a quarter million dollars in invested capital for minority businesses; that is, fifteen times the initial outlay. Church related organizations with small business investment expertise may want to establish their own MESBIC's.[4] The Presbyterian Economic Development Corporation is considering doing so. On the other hand, a church may want to invest in groups, such as the Interracial Council for Business Opportunity,[5] which are developing their own MESBIC's and already have qualified staffs. As we will discuss later in the chapter, there are many differences of opinion about the value of the "black capitalism" which MESBIC seems to foster, especially when the businesses which it spawns are very small ones. But MESBIC is only one of several options for the investor willing to risk his capital to spur economic growth, and, if the project succeeds later, to realize a significant yield. Several churches, including some boards of the United Church of Christ, have explored many minority-owned business opportunities and invested in some of them. This is PEDCO's major area of involvement.[6]

[4] It should be noted, however, that a MESBIC begun with the minimum sum may well have a difficult time getting started and sustaining itself.

[5] Founded in 1963 as a nonprofit corporation by the New York Metropolitan Council of the American Jewish Congress and the Urban League of Greater New York. National Offices are at 110 East 23rd Street, New York, New York 10010.

[6] See its first Annual Report, available by writing PEDCO, 475 Riverside Drive, New York, N. Y. 10027.

HIGH-RISK AND LOW-RETURN INVESTMENTS

Direct investments in depressed areas of the economy may often involve higher than usual risks and may not offer the potential for normal yield or return. Many co-operative developments in minority areas will return much of the profit to the local community if the venture succeeds, but will leave the investor without his principal if it does not. Here the distinction between a "grant" and an "investment" is less clear. The social impact of such funding, however, can be very great. If, for example, a community organization builds two supermarkets and a specified percentage of the profit is turned over to local community groups, the investor cannot be expected to receive a high return in any event. But the benefit to the community which such an arrangement involves would be highly significant and here many of the arguments against "black capitalism" are vitiated.

THEOLOGICAL AND ETHICAL ISSUES
INVOLVED IN CREATIVE INVESTMENT

Creative investment will probably involve the church in the very hardest ethical and social issues now facing the society. The church investor who has the option of supporting low-income housing in the inner city or of supporting groups which are concentrating on the purchase of all-white apartments in the suburbs and integrating them will face the same tough questions which churchmen on the program-allocation boards have been facing in recent years. The investor who has the choice of supporting programs which concentrate on the development of minority-owned business in the ghetto or in all-white areas must ask the hardest questions about the meaning of minority economic development.[7] The churchmen who support many small black businessmen rather than a large, cooperative, minority-owned business venture which has the potential of hiring a great number of employees is confronted with basic questions of economic policy which, in turn, cannot be divorced from the knottiest of ethical and theological issues. The investor with the option of supporting either a new economic initiative by a group of indigenous people in a foreign country or an American firm providing technology and capital on a large scale for world economic development, whose profits will return to entrepreneurs in this country, is encountering the hardest questions of international economics. It is in these situations that the differences between, for example, the "Christ of culture" and the "Christ transforming culture" churchmen may be telling. Nevertheless the church cannot back away from these questions in these times. If the total church is to have a guiding inner logic, then these ques-

[7] On this point see William F. Haddad and G. Douglas Pugh, eds., *Black Economic Development* (Englewood Cliffs, 1969). Also relevant are Theodore L. Cross, *Black Capitalism: Strategy for Business in the Ghetto* (there is a trenchant critical review of this book by Charles Silberman in the August, 1970 *Fortune*), and Robert Browne, "Toward Making Black Power Real Power," in *The Black Manifesto,* ed. Robert S. Lecky and H. Elliott Wright (New York, 1969).

tions belong in the investment boardroom as much as they belong on the church's social concerns committee.

SHOULD THE CHURCH DO IT, OR SHOULD THE CHURCH ENABLE OTHERS TO DO IT?

The creative investment field raises another set of complex questions. Should the church attempt to develop the administrative processes which will be needed in order to make informed "creative investment" decisions, or should it invest in or loan to other groups whose goals are similar to its own? An example will suggest why there is no easy answer here. The National Corporation for Housing Partnerships (NCHP), Washington, D.C., is an important creative investment opportunity. It is a quasi-public corporation which sells shares to private groups (100,000 is the minimum commitment, although it may be paid over a four-year period) which will combine management and construction expertise in housing development, seed money, and capital. It is also a center for processing housing initiatives and similar activities which spur the construction of low- and middle-income housing, particularly in the inner-city. It takes advantage of various government funding programs which support housing (including section 236 of the 1967 Housing and Urban Development Act, for example). A number of insurance companies participating in the insurance industry's Urban Investment Program as well as corporations and unions have recently invested relatively heavily in this corporation. By

June, 1970, 265 subscribers had subscribed $42 million, but capital is still needed. NCHP is, most likely, a safe investment, but the yield will probably not be high.

However, the same funds could be used to provide seed money, for example, to a local church or church group which is willing to use some of its property holdings to erect low-income housing in its area. Let us say that the local church faces a stiff fight with the local zoning board to have the land rezoned for multiple-dwelling units in an area where the citizens are unhappy about both the extra tax burdens and the effects of the change in the area's racial composition, which the housing development would involve. In the decision to rezone, many issues, such as the "inner-city" versus "suburban" solutions to the present crises, hang in the balance. They also involve difficult questions about whether the church as an institution will itself lead in some of the important social developments, or whether it will provide the means whereby those outside the church can lead them. Take another example—this time real rather than hypothetical. The Presbyterian Economic Development Corporation heard that an Alabama black man from George Wallace's home county was buying timberland which he wanted to clear himself. He had secured a loan from a local white "friend," but the "friend" later tried to force him to hire a contractor to clear the land. The black man refused and lost his loan; then he tried to get the loan from a local bank. When the bank refused, PEDCO came upon the scene. It persuaded the New York bank, for which the Alabama bank was a correspondent, to try to persuade the Southern bank to make the loan. It refused. PEDCO then deposited an amount equivalent to the loan in the bank and co-signed the loan. The Alabama bank finally decided to make what is, purportedly, its first major loan to a black man. The land is being cleared, the bank is receiving regular payment on its loan; and PEDCO feels it has broken the color line in yet one more American institution, something which would not have happened if it had made the loan directly. What is the role of the church in periods of social crisis? The American churches will not all give the same answers; but creative investment decisions will raise the question in its most difficult form. That is part and parcel of the challenge.

WHERE TO FIND OUT ABOUT CREATIVE INVESTMENT OPPORTUNITIES

The following is a very incomplete list of possible sources of information:

1. The Presbyterian Economic Development Corporation, 475 Riverside Drive, New York, N.Y. 10027 This is an independent corporation established by the United Presbyterians to manage some of the unrestricted funds which the 1968 General Assembly of the Church mandated to be spent in higher-risk, lower-return ventures. One fifth of its investments or loans has been in the area of housing; two fifths in the area of minority economic development; and

two fifths in securities of banks with strong minority loan records which send PEDCO semi-annual reports on their progress in making such loans. A copy of PEDCO's annual report will provide one model for churches considering such a program, although it should be noted that not all Presbyterians consider this effort to be an unqualified success.

2. The Cooperative Assistance Fund, 1325 Massachusetts Avenue (Suite 303), Washington, D.C. 20005

   This fund welcomes church investment and anticipates reasonable security and return, but is not yet prepared to offer yearly distribution (although such a program is being considered). It was initiated by the Taconic Foundation and has received support from the following foundations: Ford, New York, New World, Field, Norman, Ellis Phillips, Rockefeller Bros., and Sachem. The fund is concentrating on demonstration projects likely to produce institutional change.

3. Mutual Real Estate Investment Trust (MREIT), 41 East Forty-second Street, New York, N.Y.

   MREIT is a symbolic program attempting both to show that integrated housing efforts can be successful and to do something substantive to spur integrated housing. As noted, it buys apartment houses with all-white tenants, and integrates them. This has been done in several states. MREIT has at times paid cash distribution at a rate of three percent to its stockholder. Among the churches and church-related organizations which have invested in MREIT are the United Christian Missionary Society of the Disciples of Christ, the Episcopal Diocese of Missouri, COEMAR of the United Presbyterian Church of Chicago, Priests of the Holy Cross of South Bend, Indiana, and many Unitarian churches.

4. Interracial Council for Business Opportunity (ICBO), 110 East Twenty-third Street, New York, N.Y. 10010
ICBO offers the investor several social investment options, including a guaranty loan fund, a "Capital Opportunities Corporation," and a MESBIC (described above). It has been supported by the Rockefeller, Ford, New York, and other foundations.

5. Government Agencies
Information concerning government programs can be obtained through the U.S. Department of Housing and Urban Development, Washington, D.C. 20410. Especially relevant are three H.U.D. books: 4442.1 (on rental housing for lower income families; Section 236 of the 1968 housing law); F.H.A. 4400.9 (house ownership assistance for lower-income families, Section 235 (i) of the 1968 housing law); and F.H.A. 4400.22 (on multifamily rehabilitation). Write also to the Small Business Administration, Investment Division, 1441 First Street

Northwest, Washington, D.C. 20416 (especially relevant here are the MESBIC materials).

This obviously represents an inadequate listing of creative investment opportunities. Attention will be given to the need to develop an "information bank" to provide and disseminate a complete listing to socially concerned investors in chapter 7.[8] However, some research organs are now being developed which will help the investor looking for investment opportunities in minority development projects to know at least what is available. *Urban Enterprise,* a biweekly periodical published by the Urban Research Corporation, 5464 South Shore Drive, Chicago, Ill., is one such source. Annual subscriptions to it cost $50. Several church investors have found it a primary source of information. *Business and Society* calls itself a "biweekly report on Business and Social Responsibility." It tends to stress business responsibility efforts by big business, but on occasion reports on new enterprise efforts. Annual subscriptions to it are $75, and information about it is obtainable through MRM Publishing Co., Inc., 235 East Seventy-second Street, New York, N.Y. 10021. Further, a list of black business directories is included in a recent article in the *Harvard Business Review* (May-June 1970) entitled, "White Help for Black Business," by Michael Brower and Doyle Little.

The church investor will not only need to examine the

---

[8] It should be stressed that mention of any of the above projects, funds, or programs should not be construed to reflect investment recommendation.

specific options mentioned and those obtained from other sources for both their compatibility with his goals and their financial stability; he will also need to examine the restrictions on the funds he seeks to invest with social purpose to determine which of the social investment options suggested in this and the preceding chapter are possible for him. The next chapter will, hopefully, provide a framework for that analysis.

III
THE DEVELOPMENT OF SOCIALLY RESPONSIBLE INVESTMENT POLICIES IN THE CHURCHES

The church investor who seeks to implement any or all of the options described in the previous two chapters must, on the one hand, be cognizant of a range of legal and institutional questions which may inhibit his actions. On the other hand, he should not underestimate his potential to have important social and moral impact. We will begin the introduction to this section by examining the second statement.

Is the church poor, or is it wealthy? Strangely, the answer is "both." Ask any denominational executive, clergyman or member of a church board of trustees and he will tell you that not only has church membership leveled off in recent years, but in most cases the rate of church giving has also slackened and even fallen off.[1] In a time of significant inflation and increasingly heavy demands for church expenditures, these statistics do not bode well for the church. With or without the evolution of social investment policies (which may or may not be very costly), a reordering of church budget priorities is in the wind, if it is not already underway.[2]

Nevertheless, the church is, in simple dollar terms, wealthy. Estimates of church wealth vary greatly. While churches have certainly not been anxious to divulge their total holdings (and are usually not required to do so by law), reliable estimates have been difficult to develop in part because the church's wealth is held by countless different groups, in many different forms (property, stocks, bonds, commercial interests, for example), and under hundreds of different types of arrangement. Equally important, accounting procedures are anything but uniform. The United Church of Christ's Committee on Financial Investments, trying to develop investment criteria, had to develop its own categories in order to get a grasp of nothing more than the securities holdings of that church's large boards and conferences. A further com-

[1] See *The Yearbook of American Churches,* 1970, Constant H. Jacquet, Jr., ed. (New York, 1970).

[2] The best recent discussion of this point is in L. E. Schaller's "New-Style Attack on the Denominational Budget," *The Christian Century,* January 21, 1970.

plication is the question of "what counts" as church wealth: e.g., how church-related must a church-related college be to be considered a financial asset?

Despite the difficulties, estimates have been made. Martin A. Larson, the researcher who has developed the best techniques for such calculations, first estimated church wealth at $100 billion in 1965; by 1969 with new research methods he had revised the estimate upward to almost $164 billion (including annual contributions).[3]

The question concerning us in the book, however, is how much of that "incalculable" sum is held in investments? *The Wall Street Journal* attempted such a study in 1967 but gave up the effort after realizing that the three billion dollar total at which it had arrived was just a start. Indeed, a recent as yet unreleased study by one reputable church organization studied only the securities holdings of only *some* of the major boards of *seven* denominations (not including the two largest in the country) but nevertheless documents investment holdings in excess of $3 billion. Larson and Lowell estimate Protestant and Catholic investments generally (here including investment property as well as securities) at $21 billion. No figures were given on investment assets of Jewish groups. Although it is true that some of the estimates might be high, many observers point out that almost all previous calcula-

[3] See his *Church Wealth and Business Income* (New York, 1965) and *Praise the Lord for Tax Exemption,* written with C. Stanley Lowell (Washington-New York, 1969). D. B. Robertson's *Should the Churches Be Taxed* (Philadelphia, 1968) also makes an effort to estimate church wealth.

tions have vastly underrated, not overrated, church assets. Obviously, then, we are discussing in this book a considerable amount of money.

Where does it all come from? Church investment funds are derived from a variety of sources, but relatively little is from the collection plate. Most of this money is spent rather quickly. It is true that after several steps, plate offerings and annual pledges sometimes become investment funds. For example, a church building drive fifty years ago, funded through Sunday collections, may have bought church property since leased and now held as an investment. In addition, collections help meet church budgets which, in turn, pay ministers, and ministers and their churches pay church pension board premiums. Although this is much less frequently the case today, income levels in the past for many church boards exceeded budgetary needs, and these surplus funds were set aside as endowment funds. (Unrestricted funds, for which a definition will be given in the next chapter, are often derived in this way.)

While these facts and figures are of some interest, they will not tell the social investor much about what initiatives are possible. A multitude of endowment arrangements, gift restrictions, and other limitations spawn a great many difficult questions, many of which are formidable and complex legal ones which the church must examine as it moves into the social investment arena. The generalizations offered in chapter 5 will not completely elucidate even the various limitations which exist. They are even less adequate for helping each individual social investor or church board estimate what is the potential for his efforts.

The legal questions are just part of the story, however. There is a wide range of institutional inhibitions about actually applying the *raison d'être* of the church to the investment aspect of its operations. Some suggestions will be made in chapter 6 to "structure" social criteria into the investment decision-making processes, but the actual structures will be almost as different as the organizations which set them up. Finally, the dearth of information relevant to developing social investment criteria will be discussed; the suggestions here are more for what should be done to help inform the social investor than indices for present involvement.

5

The Institutional Element: Resilient and Not So Resilient Barriers to Social Investment Policies

This chapter is divided into four sections. The first schematizes the basic categories in which church funds are held. The second section presents some proposals for new ways of thinking about these basic categories which could remove roadblocks which have frustrated attempts to free church funds for social investment purposes. The third focuses on the anomalous pension board funds. The fourth looks at some more general, but no less difficult, institutional issues which impede social investment practice.

CATEGORIES OF CHURCH
INVESTMENT FUNDS

Most church funds can be said to fall under one of three categories, each of which must receive separate treatment.

Unrestricted Funds. Church boards (especially mission boards) often hold a significant portion of unrestricted funds. These are funds upon which the donor(s) placed no legal restrictions as to the purpose for which the funds are to be used, the way in which the funds are to be invested, or the rate at which the funds are to be spent. The basic restriction which pertains to these funds is that they must be spent for purposes consistent with the "corporate purposes" of the agencies which hold them. For example, the United Church Board for World Ministries has a revised charter which gives it a very broad mandate specifying corporate powers broad enough to carry on virtually any social investment activity such a church agency might choose to undertake *with its unrestricted funds.* An incorporated church board established solely to promote the physical and spiritual health of the people in Lima, Peru, however, would be significantly more limited in deploying its unrestricted funds.[1]

The use of unrestricted funds is restrained in one other way. All charitable institutions which benefit from tax-

[1] It is possible to amend corporate charters. Church organizations do this on a regular basis. Indeed, there is a trend among them to develop and obtain state approval for broad corporate purposes and powers.

exempt status (thus allowing donors tax-deductible gifts to the agency and freeing the agency from most tax obligations) must use their funds in accordance with section 501(c) of the Internal Revenue Code and with the similar tax provisions in the incorporating state.[2]

Unrestricted funds function as endowment. They are available for any use permitted by the charter of the agency holding them and may be spent as quickly or slowly as the church board wishes to spend them. When they are retained as endowment funds it is to provide program-funding over time for the agency. They are *investment* funds by choice, not by legal necessity. Obviously then, the church may most actively pursue a social investment policy with these funds. The United Presbyterian Church (USA) recognized this when its 1968 General Assembly instructed the boards and agencies of the Assembly, including the United Presbyterian Foundation, to make thirty percent of their unrestricted funds available for investment in housing and businesses in low- and middle-income areas, and acknowledged that some such investments would involve a higher risk and lower return.[3] The Committee on Financial Investments of the United Church of Christ made a somewhat analogous recommendation to the boards and conferences of that church in the fall of 1970.

[2] No attention is given in this book to the many questions involving church taxation. The reader is referred to the burgeoning literature on this subject, including D. B. Robertson, *Should the Churches Be Taxed?* (Philadelphia, 1968).

[3] See Appendix B.

Restricted Funds. "Restricted" here refers to funds which are, in some way, available only for purposes narrower than the most general purpose of the agency holding them. There is one type of "restricted" gift which we will not discuss at length. A donor may direct that his bequest be used for a specific program within the more general program of the church. An example here is a donor who specified that his gift be used to support a particular effort in the education of African schoolchildren, but does not specify how quickly it is to be spent. Social investment questions can arise, however, if the church agency decides to invest this type of gift rather than expend it immediately. If so, it appears that the board may be legally obligated to spend only the amount given for that purpose. However, the board may be obligated to spend that part of the yield which compensates for inflation.

The two most frequently encountered restrictions, however, are the following, where the donor and/or the church agency itself has specified how the gift or bequest is to be used as an investment:

1. In some rather infrequent cases the donor may give specific instructions about the investment management of his gift. He may, for example, specify that a given security is not to be sold, or is not to be sold except under certain conditions. Alternatively, and this is a boon to the social investor, he may specify that some of

the rules which normally bind a trustee of restricted funds are inapplicable in regard to his gift.[4]

2. In most cases, "restricted funds" are those which are mandatorily held as endowment (as investments) and only the income (the investment return) which the gift produces can be spent. The person placing the restriction may specify that that "income" is to be spent for purposes within the general corporate charter mandate or for specific areas within the agency's more general work.

Most of the investment funds held by churches (with the possible exception of the pension boards, as will be discussed) fall into this second category of the more general category of "restricted funds."

What are the duties of the fiduciary (that is, the legally responsible person or group of the recipient agency) in investing these funds? The traditional view which has guided the investment policies of most churches both in regard to investment of restricted funds and unrestricted funds is that one set forth in trust law, and more specifically in a doctrine known as the prudent man rule. Whether or not the prudent man rule need apply to church trustees and whether it makes a difference to the interpretation of the prudent man rule that the funds in question are held by a church, a charitable trust, or corporation, will be discussed later in the chapter. Here the prudent man rule

---

[4] Further discussion of this will be offered later in the chapter.

is simply explained. (It should be stressed here that where a trustee is not seeking to attain the goals and purposes of the organization by his utilization of the options we have discussed, he will *always* be subject to the prudent man rule when he invests.)

Contrary to what some advocates of social investment policies think, trust law, at least those aspects of it relevant to our discussion, was not promulgated with the intent of hindering social progress. It was intended primarily to promote care, skill, and caution in trust management and to prevent those who manage the funds of others from using monies entrusted to their care for their own purposes rather than for the benefit of the beneficiaries which the donor specified. In earlier times, the types of investments which a "trustee" could make with someone else's money were severely limited. By most states, the prudent man rule, in varying forms, was developed to give the trustee greater flexibility in managing funds entrusted to him than he had previously had, without, at the same time, allowing him to be profligate or to use the funds for his personal gain. The following rule was then developed (though again, precisely how it limits the trustee depends upon the state law with jurisdiction over the trust) :

In making investments of trust funds the trustee is under a duty to the beneficiary . . . in the absence of provisions in the terms of the trust or of a statue otherwise providing to make such investments and only such investments as a prudent man would make of his own property having in view the preservation of the estate and the amount and regularity of income to be derived.[5]

In spelling out this statement, the authoritative legal texts in this field list care, skill, and caution as the characteristics needed for trusteeship. The trustee is instructed to consider a range of other factors including the marketability of a particular investment, the prospects for inflation, and advantages of diversifying his holdings. It is unclear whether or not it is requisite for the trustee bound by the prudent man rule to seek only maximum return with maximum safety. But one thing is clear. Where efforts to secure a social goal conflict with the protection of the benefits to be received by the beneficiaries as specified by the donor, the investor is obligated to consider the beneficiary. Generally, if the fiduciary fails to observe the law regulating his action as a trustee, he is personally liable, and may be surcharged for all or part of the amount lost by the beneficiary. Although prosecution is exceedingly rare as regards trustees of charitable institutions, the potential of liability is present. Beneficiaries, remaindermen, and/or a state official (normally the Attorney-General) may initiate litigation where violations are deemed to have occurred; the donor normally has no standing in court.

What does this mean with regard to social investment possibilities? Let's run through the options: only in rare

[5] Paragraph 227, *Restatement of the Law (Second) Trusts,* 2nd. American Law Institute, St. Paul, Minn., 1959.

cases would the protest sale of or refusal to purchase specific stock violate this provision—normally there are other "prudent" options unless the practices of a *very* great number of corporations were being protested. Although, again, it would be rare, decisions to purchase stock in corporations deemed socially progressive could possibly be imprudent. To date, no proxy contest motivated by social concern known to the author could have been reliably projected to have seriously damaged a corporation's ability to make a profit. Hence the "prudent" investor could have voted either way. Under the new Court of Appeals Ruling such options might conceivably be offered in the future, but this too is unclear and perhaps doubtful. Some in the profession are now debating whether a trustee could make a proxy vote decision costly to the corporation in the "short" run, but probably beneficial to it in the "long" run *and* beneficial to the welfare of the beneficiary. Pollution would be a case in point. The health of a beneficiary residing in New York City could be projected to be jeopardized by polluting automobiles to such an extent that his trustee would be prudent to vote for pollution abatement stockholder proposals even if the success of the proposal would weaken the next quarter's dividends. This is especially true if the trustee projects that, in the long run, corporations with good pollution records will be the profitable ones, and there exists the intention to hold the stock overtime. The trustees of New York City investment funds apparently gave a similar rationale in voting for the Project GM proposals (although, again, these proposals, as suggested, did not involve certain cost). Somewhat analogous arguments could be made as regards use of the corporate persuasion and derivative suit options.

Most problems arise in the area of creative investment. Assume for the moment that the charitable trustee investing church funds has the same obligations as does any other trustee (a premise questioned later in the chapter). An example will make this point clear. The Unitarian-Universalist Church, having no significant unrestricted funds to invest, mandated a social investment committee to attempt to invest $500,000 of the Association's restricted funds in socially worthwhile projects. "The Final Report and Recommendations of the Committee on Social Responsibility and Investments" issued in spring, 1970, details the problems faced by a group which spent a great deal of time attempting to find creative investment opportunities which met the test of the traditional prudent man —and were consistently frustrated. They found investment opportunities for only a fraction of that total. While the situation creating this result will certainly improve as new programs for economic development are established and become stronger, creative investment opportunities at present are, perhaps, relatively few where the prudent man rule, as normally understood, applies. It should be noted that there are now discussions in the federal government about developing legislation which will provide guarantees for organizational investors who invest in high-risk and lower-return projects or institutions for social investment purposes. When and if such legislation is proposed and passed, restricted funds, now unavailable, may well become available.

Contract Funds. Most generally, contract funds are received subject to a contract requiring the performance of certain acts by the recipient. When such funds are invested, they are commonly invested in the same way as restricted funds; but this need not be the case unless that contract itself so requires or the funds involved in the contract are themselves "restricted." Attention is drawn to these funds as a separate category, since they are often overlooked as a distinct type of investment resource. The social investor will want to be aware of the specific restrictions in the contract regulating the investment of such funds;[6] he may also explore the possibility of persuading the parties to the contract to make it more available for social investment options by changing its terms. It is impossible to specify generally what options for social investment are open to investors managing contract funds; only knowledge of the specific contract(s) can reveal that. But this area should not be overlooked by the socially conscious investor.

ANOTHER LOOK AT RESTRICTIONS: HOW RESTRICTIVE DO THEY HAVE TO BE?

There are two basic options for increasing the funds available for social investment purposes. The first involves

---

[6] Sometimes there are several sets of contracts.

a variety of ways in which restricted funds may be moved to the unrestricted funds column; the second, discussed in possibility 6, involves another look at the restrictions applicable to restricted funds held by church agencies and governed by the prudent man rule.

1. One of these is quite easy, involves no legal impediments at all, and is an essential first step for the social investor seeking additional funds for his efforts. In many church boards, funds are "restricted" not because the donor has placed restrictions upon them, but because the board of trustees of the church organization has placed them there. An example will help. A local church receives an unrestricted bequest of $50,000. Although there is no immediate need to expend the bequest at the time it is received, the church envisages a continuing need for church maintenance. It thus designates the income derived from the bequest to be spent only for the purpose of maintaining the church. These funds are, then, placed in the category of restricted funds and invested along with its other restricted funds according to the applicable rules. If the church board or its successors is seeking equity for creative investment initiatives (or for any other purpose), it may remove the restriction because *it* originally specified the restriction. These then become unrestricted funds. Many church boards hold large amounts of such "self-restricted" funds.

2. For restricted funds which have been held for a long period of time, there is another possibility. In a recent study, *The Law and the Lore of Endowment Funds,* two

eminent legal scholars, William Cary[7] and Craig Bright, endorsed by a battery of others, argued that in most cases a trustee may, with due concern for inflation and protection of the principal, consider the capital gains on stocks not simply as principal but as income (along with dividend return). Another example will help here. If a donor leaves a gift of $5,000, requiring only that it be invested, and that money is invested in stock, it is possible that over a twenty-year period, the market value of the gift could rise to $20,000. If in that period of time inflation averages five percent a year, for example, then the gift's value should be $10,000, under the inflated condition. But the other $10,000 may now be considered "unrestricted" funds. Several educational institutions are now treating their capital gains as income in this way in order to allow them to take advantage of stocks with low-dividend yields, but good capital gains prospects. The social investor, however, may increase his "unrestricted fund" total using this rationale. Accounting procedures in this option may be time-consuming, but potentially very important. The cautious investor will want to secure a copy of the Cary-Bright report for himself, which he may do by writing the Ford Foundation.[8]

3. Churches and other nonprofit institutions have long been plagued by donor-restricted gifts whose purpose they can no longer fulfill, or whose purpose has become totally

[7] Cary is perhaps the leading authority on corporate law in America and former head of the Securities Exchange Commission.

[8] 320 East Forty-third Street, New York, N.Y. 10017.

irrelevant to the life and goals of the agency. In such cases, churches must (and do!) obtain approval from the courts to change the purpose of the gift to a purpose which is relevant or possible (the funds remain restricted, but are now able to fulfill another purpose specified by the court). Another hypothetical example will explain the procedure. A donor left a bequest in the 1940's to a mission board to care for young children paralyzed by polio-myelitis in a specific region of the country. In order to extend the effectiveness of the gift, he specified that only the income and not the principal could be used. By the 1960's, no children had polio in the specified region as a result of effective vaccination programs. Using *cy pres,* the church had the restriction altered. In those cases where judicial authorities change the monies from one restricted purpose to another, it is conceivable that this change would be accompanied by liberalized treatment of the restrictions governing use of principal.

4. One complicated but potentially useful possibility has not, to the author's knowledge, been tried. It involves "guaranteeing" restricted funds with "unrestricted" funds to increase the monies open to social investment possibilities. Here collateral could shore up any loss in either principal or income. Obviously, collateral must be carefully protected, and legal opinion must be obtained about what is sufficient for the social investment initiative under discussion. While guarantee could be provided by unrestricted investment funds, it could also be provided by an innovative use of church property—either real property

investments or the land and building of the house of worship itself. Three possibilities exist here:

    a. That the land ownings or church property be used directly as collateral;

    b. That the property be mortgaged to obtain collateral funds; or,

    c. That the church sell existing property (church land-ownings exclusive of the property on which the local church sits are extensive) and either invest socially or keep the property as a hedge against losses on restricted funds invested for social purpose.

Some local churches have mortgaged their properties and used the derived income for direct grants to worthy projects; the social investment option is an alternative possibility and might be more attractive since it would not necessarily involve a loss in assets.

5. It has recently been proposed that *incorporated* church agencies do not really hold any "restricted" funds, and hence that the prudent man rule is not always applicable. It is true that some form of the prudent man rule seems to apply unequivocally to the restricted funds of charitable *trusts*. But there may well be a distinction of great consequence between a charitable trust and a charitable corporation. On the basis of a number of court decisions, Cary and Bright, in *The Law and the Lore of Endowment Funds* cited above, argue that

. . . where the issue involves the investment of funds, accounting for their use or other aspect of administration or housekeeping, the courts show a marked tendency to apply corporate principles rather than trust principles, in order to accord charitable corporations a maximum degree of flexibility in their operations.[9]

Put simply, this means that corporate law generally accords an incorporated body "absolute ownership" of the funds it holds. According to Cary and Bright, adherence to this doctrine varies from state to state; Massachusetts is more reluctant to accept it than is New York, for example.[10] But, significantly, Cary and Bright conclude that the courts tend to choose the principles of law (trust or corporate) which it applies, depending upon "the result which the court deems it socially desirable to obtain." [11] To the author's knowledge, use of this doctrine for social investment purposes (that is, using the "absolute ownership" doctrine as the basis upon which to consider all funds "unrestricted") has never been tested in court. A church interested in pursuing it would have to do so in court or at least secure expert legal opinion. Reasons other than social investment ones exist for using this doctrine. First, it would simplify and perhaps end the use of costly *cy pres* procedures. It would also simplify and quite possibly eliminate the administrative procedures needed to keep track of a variety of restrictions and to separate restricted from unrestricted funds.

The experienced investor will notice that the ways of

[9] P. 27.

[10] All states accept it more readily when the donor's intent is obscure.

[11] *Law and Lore*, p. 18.

removing restrictions from restricted funds already discussed here will involve more administrative effort than now is required in investment management. The investor would have to go through an extended process, sometimes involving litigation or pre-litigation procedures in order to increase his unrestricted holdings. Furthermore, he might have to establish several different funds, each with *different* investment criteria. If the Cary-Bright doctrine is accepted, however, church investors could more readily get down to the hard decisions of knowing how much and what of their invested funds they want to invest for social purposes.

6. Should "possibility number five" turn out to be incorrect, it will be necessary to think carefully about how the prudent man rule does and does not apply—in its strict form—to charitable institutions. The issue in its sharpest form is: is a trustee of a charitable trust required to be prudent in the same way and about the same things as a trustee of any other trust? The answer to this question will hinge on whether one views "prudence" as it is used in the law as a "formal" or "material" concept. Put more simply, must a trustee be prudent (skillful, cautious, and careful) solely in the pursuit of maximum safety, maximum return, or is he to be prudent in whatever he is required or allowed to be prudent about? If it is the latter, then the purposes and goals of the institution and/or beneficiary for whom he is investing become matters which he may prudently seek to realize.

A great deal has been said in recent years about the

suggestion that there is an "extra dimension"—a social dimension—to the task of the trustee of a charitable organization. The final report of the Committee on Social Responsibility and Investments of the Unitarian-Universalist Association states that Austin Wakeman Scott, one of (if not *the*) leading trust authorities in the country, told the committee counsel that he believes there is such an "extra dimension," although he did not attempt to define it.

Surely a trustee of a charitable trust must be certain that his trust's investments do not support or acquiesce in violations of public policy.[12] (It must be admitted, however, that few terms are so vague in the law as "public policy"—or perhaps that is a boon!). The more basic question before us, however, is whether the "extra-dimension" alluded to allows involvement in the more affirmative of the initiatives which have been suggested in chapters 3 and 4. Does it allow a projected loss of two percent, of three percent, of four percent? Does it mean

[12] In thinking about this area, careful scrutiny of the legal texts will be required. Although the author does not presume to be competent to develop a brief on the subject, he suggests that special attention be given to the following paragraphs from the *Restatement of the Law (Second) Trusts:* 193, 227, 377c, 381, 382, 391. The most recent—and perhaps the most sophisticated discussion of legal restraints as they apply to social investment efforts is that set forth in the legal section of the forthcoming monograph on university investments to which reference was made in chapter 2. This section, written by John G. Simon, Professor of Law at Yale, provides justification only for the specific guidelines for "corporate element" social investment initiatives by *universities*. It does, however, open up some important new perspectives on trust law to which churches may find analogues applicable to their own legal situations.

that an investor can make social-impact investments a little more—or much more—risky than normal ones?

The Unitarian-Universalist Association Committee made an effort—or started to make an effort—to find out. It asked the Attorney General's office in Massachusetts (a state which has tended toward strict trust law interpretation) whether it saw an extra dimension. It did not, and indicated that it would oppose any suit which attempted to establish one. The lines were drawn, then, and the next move was up to the UUA. It asked other denominations to join it—or at least help defray the litigation costs which this test would have involved. The UUA was unable to find allies, however, and the issue was dropped.

If social investment is to become a concept which informs the investment of most or all church funds, then some church or other charitable institution will have to try the test case(s). There is a case to be made, and perhaps won. Surely it is worth the effort and expense if the churches are serious about this new area of mission.

Pension Boards. The discussion just completed probably applies to most church agencies. One anomalous type of church board, however, needs separate discussion. Church pension boards, like other pension boards in the country, have generally been established to provide various sorts of post-employment protection and income for the clergy and church layworkers. If the churches hope to lead other societal institutions toward employment of the options discussed earlier, church pension boards may have an important role. Adolph Berle[13] estimates that the present $30 billion in pension board holdings in the nation will probably level off in about twenty years to between $70 and $80 billion and will control between 20 and 45 percent of the stockholdings in major U.S. companies. Berle projects that this power will lie in the hands of a relatively few pension trustees (mostly banks and insurance companies) since the pensionary has virtually no property rights in the control of the pension trust. Berle also expects that, as their power grows, pension trustees will no longer remain passive and receptive but will become quite active in returning "owner" control to the stockholder.[14]

Those interested in the issues raised in the first chapter will be concerned about how pension trustees will use that power or look for ways to disperse it. Legislation proposed for the Administration by Senator Jacob Javits[15] and currently being considered by the U.S. Senate is attempting to place restrictions upon pension board trustees to make certain that those funds are not used with indiscretion or for the trustees' personal interest. The device

[13] "Economic Power and the Free Society."

[14] Congressman Wright Patman has become increasingly concerned about this concentration of power, and a subcommittee of his Committee on Banking and Currency has published two massive volumes on the issue: *Commercial Banks and Their Trust Activities: Emerging Influence on the American Economy,* July 9, 1968. See also, Paul P. Harbecht, *Pension Funds and Their Economic Power* (New York, 1959) and "Is Trust Power Excessive," *The New York Times,* Business and Financial Section (3), October 11, 1970, p. 1.

[15] The Employees Benefit Protection Act S. 3589.

being used is the prudent man rule. In response to a letter from the author, Senator Javits requested the Solicitor Designate of the Department of Labor, the agency which had prepared the bill, to judge whether the legislation would inhibit pension trustees in developing social investment policies if they used some of the options discussed in chapters 3 and 4.

The response of the Solicitor Designate, Peter G. Nash, must be considered advisory only, since the Labor Department will issue interpretative bulletins if the bill passes, and even then the courts will have to provide the authoritative interpretation of the law on specific issues. However, using the 1969 GM proxy contests as an example, Mr. Nash ventured that pension board members would not violate the proposed act in voting for or against the Campaign GM proposals. As to whether investments of a less than minimum risk and lower than maximum return could be made if the purpose was a social goal, the Solicitor Designate responded as follows:

As with all investments, the basic requirement is the same, i.e., the investment must be prudent. I think the rule of prudence allows a wide range to decision-makers. Whether it is prudent to make a particular investment depends upon a reasonable assessment of the circumstances at the time. An immediate high yield would not necessarily make an investment prudent. And weighing in the balance the long-term interests of the plan's participants and their families would certainly not be imprudent.

This letter seems to suggest that what church pension boards do in response to the social investment issue could serve an exemplary function. (It should be noted here that the new law would regulate only some church pension plans.)

There appear to be two basic types of church pension funds: (1) those governed by a trustee relationship between the church board and a bank, insurance company, or other independent trustee; and (2) those managed by a church investment board itself. These should be looked at separately.

1. The Pension and Investment Plan of the National Council of Churches is an example of the first type. The trustee of the plan is Morgan Guaranty and Trust Company, which the General Board of the N.C.C. retains and may remove. The bank's trust department has discretion as to what stocks that plan holds (within wide limits as to classification of securities), how it votes the proxies, etc. The General Board may amend the trustee agreement so long as (1) the trustee agrees, (2) the amendment does not violate Internal Revenue Code laws relevant to such pension trusts, and (3) the amendment does not divert funds from other than the exclusive benefit of participating employees. In 1963 such an amendment was made which disallowed the trustee from investing in companies which manufacture and sell alcohol and tobacco. (This restriction does not apply to that part of the pension's funds which are in commingled funds—that is, funds

which represent a pool of trust accounts for the purpose of investment management.)[16]

Such a pension plan model offers relatively few possibilities for social investment initiatives. Consider the following example. The Investment Committee which handles the National Council's general investment funds voted for Project GM in the proxy contest in spring, 1970. The bank trustees, however, may quite possibly have voted the pension funds of the National Council for GM's management. Under the present regulations, the Investment Board could only have advised the bank of its preference on this issue (and did not do that). An amendment could perhaps be devised whereby the bank would turn over proxies to the N.C.C. on specified issues—if the bank agreed to such an amendment, and it did not violate any other rule relevant to the trust.

As regards other social investment options, such a plan allows little leeway. Protest sale of stock would be impossible, management persuasion might be less effective since the N.C.C. does not actually control investment and derivative suits could be initiated only by the bank trustee. The one social investment aspect of the existing agreement (that relating to alcohol and tobacco producers)

[16] This raises another point, although space limitations prevent an extensive discussion of it. Briefly, many trusts are held in commingled funds in order to give the investment manager a larger pool to work with. These funds consist of the holdings of several, or a great number of, trusts which have similar restrictions. If the social investor is to be free to utilize his social criteria with regard to specific companies, he may have to remove his trust from such commingled funds.

could probably be extended only as regards a classification of stock (a whole industry) and would therefore be quite imprecise. The N.C.C. could suggest "creative investment" options alluded to in the Solicitor Designate's letter, but these would not be mandatory for the trustee. Only a new trust agreement, which would still be subject to severe limitations and which could be occasioned only by a removal of the existing trustee, would allow stronger N.C.C. initiatives in the creative investment area. Whether such a change in trustees would be advantageous to all concerned is questionable.

But all this in turn suggests another type of social investment option: *trustee persuasion.* If the N.C.C. and similar pension boards began to raise social investment issues with the independent trustees with whom they have agreements, some needed "fresh air" might be let into trust departments of banks and insurance companies. The informal "leverage" which such church pension or investment boards have with those trust departments might not be an insignificant factor and might have far-reaching consequences as the power of pension trustees grows.

2. The Pension Boards of the United Church of Christ represent the other pension board model.[17] Many more options are available in this model. Here the church's own investors retain control of the investment management under an implicit contract with the churches and employees contributing to the church's pension plan. While the

[17] The General Board of Pensions of the United Methodist Church appears to be another example of this model.

prudent man rule normally governs the pension board's management of its funds in this model, some church pension boards have begun to exercise some ownership prerogatives in corporations in which they hold stock. One of the guidelines for the General Pension Board of The United Methodist Church specifies the following social and moral goals: "These funds are not knowingly invested in enterprises out of accord with the general social and moral aims of the church and, where feasible, investments are made in support of such aims." But the "implied contract" status of this pension board model opens other still unexplored possibilities. Many clergy and lay workers desire the maximum protection of benefits for retirement and would not be interested in social investment efforts. Others, however, would probably like to see the money which they and their church contribute to the pension fund used for relatively aggressive social investment purposes during their working years. Although they have only recently been given serious attention, some proposals have been made that church pension boards structured on this model establish parallel funds, those invested in the usual way and those invested with an eye to some of the options discussed in chapters 3 and 4. Agreement to place funds in this second investment pool would have to be obtained from all those concerned (the pensionary, the church board which helps contribute to the funds, and successor beneficiaries). Initiative for such a proposal might come either from the pension boards themselves or from concerned pensionaries.

Institutional Considerations. This entire discussion has proceeded as though only legal impediments hindered churches in social investments. Although most of the objections which have been thrown up in social investment discussions have been legal, institutional impediments lie behind many of these legal arguments. Only when the dust of the legal deterrents has cleared will we be able to see the very difficult institutional decisions which have to be made. It is possible, however, to project some of them and to initiate discussion on them.

The social investing church will have to face one interesting dilemma concerning the implied "moral commitments" it has to those who have given gifts for specific purposes but whose designations are not legally binding. As we have seen, the church faces this often when it employs *cy pres* to change existing restrictions which it is no longer able to fulfill, but social investment initiatives will raise many more. The problem has two sides: (1) what can the church do to *avoid* becoming involved in decisions which require it to choose between conflicting obligations? (the obligation to respect the legally unenforceable donor's intent and the obligation to be a church relevant to new needs in a time other than that in which the gift is given); and (2) what responsibility does the church have to past donors who could not have envisaged the new needs and changing economic and political situation in which the church is now living? We will look at these two points separately.

1. Preparing for the future: The church moving into

the social investment arena must convince its members that the church of the future must be able to meet changing mission needs and priorities with flexibility and creativity. If, as Emil Brunner argued, "The church exists by mission as fire exists by burning," the church's existence will depend upon the quality of its mission, no matter how the faith-culture relationship is viewed. Christians must believe that there will be a vital and living church in the future and that every new generation will be called upon to redefine what the calling of the church is in its time, and be able to utilize its existing resources to do what it believes it must do. The vital church must persuade its members that their responsibility is to help, not stifle, the generation which will follow it, and to have as much faith in the sincerity of its calling as it has in its own.

What does this mean in practical terms? If the employment of the church's funds is legally governed by corporate principles, and as Cary and Bright suggest, not trust principles, then it should make clear to the church membership that the church investment funds are of a piece and may be considered unrestricted. If this interpretation is incorrect, then the following suggestions may be helpful:

(1) that the church inform prospective contributors of the importance of receiving unrestricted funds for allowing the body of the faithful to determine at some future time where the mission of the church most needs support;

(2) that church agencies require that those restricted

gifts which they accept are restricted only to purposes consistent with the existing priorities of the church. As one church investor has put it: "There is no reason why the church should husband animals—a donor who wants to support that effort should give his money to the SPCA, not the church."

(3) that restrictions on gifts be limited to a specified period of ten years, for example, after which time they become unrestricted. This allows a donor to support a specific cause about which he is concerned, but does not tie the church to support it in perpetuity.

(4) that church agencies accept endowment gifts with the clear understanding that in some cases responsible stewardship will require that those funds be invested at less than maximum return and maximum safety so that church investment funds may be freed for mission work, even as the yield from them (albeit perhaps lower) provides the means for other aspects of the church's labor.

2. Responsibility to the past: What has already been said about the needs of a vital church in the previous section is preparatory to the difficult issue which must be faced here. The church faces a clear conflict of obligations in those cases where the donor's intent may be relatively clear but the mission needs of the church point in a different direction, and the legal impediments are no longer significant. Churchmen will differ in their response to this dilemma. Surely in cases where the original donor is

still living, efforts should be made to contact him and to explain the new legal situation, as well as to explain the new needs of the church.

From many theological perspectives, the church is probably morally bound to agreements made in the past, which are clear in intent and still possible to perform—and assuming the agreement cannot be altered by mutual consent of the concerned parties. This does not mean that many of the options discussed in the previous two chapters are ruled out for the investor who is bound by moral obligations specified in earlier restrictions. It does mean that, in many cases, full use of the most aggressive of these possibilities will be inhibited. This conflict of obligations caused by past agreements which now inhibit the most creative efforts of the churches will hopefully be an added incentive to make certain that future investors will not be inflexibly bound to agreements which the donor and the church are now making. Promise-keeping is so important an ethical category that the institutional church should think through, much more clearly than it has in the past, the promises it is willing to make.

Another way of looking at this issue argues that the donor employed the legal prerogatives available to him at the time the gift was given and in this way was depending upon the law, not the church, to enforce this desire. The author is not, however, endorsing this view.

A different range of institutional issues should receive brief mention. They also have to do with creative thinking about how the church must fulfill its mission. If, because of its social investment initiatives, the church receives less income for its program or, in extreme cases, has less endowment from which to receive income, this must not be glossed over but faced squarely. Less endowment income will mean less money for church grants, programs, etc. A living church, one whose *raison d'être* informs all its activities and which allows no split between the ethics of its money management and the ethics of its other activities, may be the kind of church which attracts continued and growing support.[18] Though some sociological evidence supports this statement, it is admittedly speculative. If social investment is as important an activity as this book has argued, then the church cannot ignore it as a new area of mission. Nor can it ignore some of the consequences of disgruntled dissidents and smaller budgets which social investment may cause. New efforts to make the church the church are always costly!

[18] On this point the author has been amazed to learn of a formal report made by a member of a large denominational board with considerable investment holdings to that board. This churchman argued that the policies of his board have always been conducted in accordance with a biblical principle, e.g., singleness of purpose. The biblical allusion was to Jesus' saying that "No one can serve two masters." (Matt. 6:24) The churchman failed to make reference, however, to the rest of the verse: "for either he will hate the one and love the other, or he will be devoted to one and despise the other. You cannot serve God and mammon." Since in the context, the investor called for single-minded pursuit of maximum return on investments, he apparently either equated maximum return, maximum yield with God or godly ways, or . . . . Singleness of institutional purpose within the constraints of applicable law and prior commitments, is, of course, something which this book has consistently argued for. The question, however, is which *raison d'être* should the church be single-minded about?

6
The Organizational and Informational Elements

How does one carry out all that has been discussed in this book, and where does one find out specifically what is going on in corporate America and in economic development? The answers here are not easy either.

THE ORGANIZATIONAL ELEMENT

Church polities differ radically; legal restrictions on who can tell whom to do what are numerous; organizations of different sizes and with different size portfolios will proceed differently. Although it is almost foolhardy, then, to counsel church organizations how to proceed in making social concerns part of their investment practice, some very general suggestions may help.

How a Church Gets Started. Someone must make a concrete decision to search for a social investment policy. Often it may be the largest corporate body with authority in the church. In the United Presbyterian Church, U.S.A., the primary decisions have been made at that denomination's General Assembly; the General Synod laid down the mandate for the United Church of Christ's committee. In churches where apostolic succession is more revered, initiative may come from the bishops. In a local church it may be the congregational meeting.

A decision to initiate the process is not the same as laying down guidelines. The larger body will probably appoint a committee to develop a proposal for the wider church. Some churches may prefer to mandate a division, office, or board of the church to lay the concrete groundwork. This committee or office will need guidance on the following types of issues:

1. Does the church want a document which will attempt to relate the church's already promulgated social policy to the investment portfolio? Or does it want a document which develops social policy as well as criteria for investment? The answer will probably depend on what the church has said in the past and how adequate those declarations are to the social investment task and the contemporary needs as the church sees them. (see chapter 2)

2. How aggressive a social investment policy is desired?

Does the church want to move very slowly or with considerable zeal? If restrictions permitted, how much might the church be willing to sacrifice in investment income? (see chapter 5)

3. Does the church's stance toward culture suggest a purity or an effectiveness model? (see chapter 2)

With these guidelines, the committee or other designated group will need time to develop a meaningful policy and a workable structural model for its policies. It will want to consider and examine the following issues:

1. How much does the church body (do the church bodies) for which the policy is being developed have in investments? What restrictions exist on those funds? What possibilities are there for removing some of them? (see chapter 5)

2. Where do the legal statutes applicable to the relevant investment funds lodge authority for investment management?

3. What structures will need to be changed or created to handle social investments?

4. What sort of additional staff time or persons will be required to do the social investment task well? (For example, staff will be required to prepare proposals and maintain contact with other institutions similarly involved.) Who would hire such a person, and to whom would he be responsible? Would he be a member of the decision-making body or attend with voice but not with vote?

5. What procedures need to be established in order to

revise the criteria developed or derived from church policies and to keep them up to date?

6. What assurances must the larger church body give to those with social investment responsibilities? Trustees for the church boards of the United Presbyterian Church, U.S.A., asked the church to face this question after the General Assembly mandated the church boards under its jurisdiction to use 30 percent of its unrestricted funds in higher-risk, lower-return investments. The trustees asked the General Assembly to hold them innocent of losses on investments made in accord with the General Assembly's directive.[1]

Models for Social Investment Decision-making. Model 1 leaves all investment decisions in existing organizational frameworks. (For some churches this may be legally necessary.) However, because investment decisions would henceforth involve considerations not previously within the scope of traditional investment management, efforts would have to be made to find and include on the existing boards additional or replacement members with expertise on social issues and the implications for investments. Persons representing diverse points of view within the church would undoubtedly enhance the acceptability of that body's decisions. Such a structure would almost certainly involve procedures for review of initiatives made. The United Church of Christ, in part because of legal and

[1] See Appendix B.

other institutional considerations, developed a model analogous to this one.

Model 2 is an option which involves the creation of a separate social investment committee or lodges social investment functions in an existing social responsibility committee. This committee could draw up, receive, vote on, and pass its proposals to the regular investment committee. A decision about the authority such a committee would have would be necessary. The advantage of this option is that a specified group of persons in the church could focus on familiarizing themselves with the various issues which social investment raises; they would not have to split their attention between regular investment decisions and socially motivated ones. This advantage is, nevertheless, its own pitfall. Important disagreements between the two committees might develop and tend to delay decisions. Establishment of committees with overlapping memberships might overcome this potential problem. The Unitarian-Universalist's committee was structured in this way.[2]

Model 3 takes social investment, especially creative options, out of the traditional investment committee altogether. This is essentially what the Presbyterians did when they created the Presbyterian Economic Develop-

[2] Neither Models 1 or 2 distinguish between the "corporate investment element" and the "creative investment element." Some churches may wish to make the split clear, leaving the corporate element to a regular investment committee and developing a separate committee to screen creative investment possibilities. Perhaps it should be the other way around. Or perhaps there should be three committees—with very clear jurisdictional instructions, of course.

ment Corporation (PEDCO) with its own separate board. They turned over a specified percentage of unrestricted funds to the new corporation which now handles their investment. While this autonomy will certainly spawn innovative employment of social investment funds, it has two drawbacks. First, it will work well only with "creative investment" possibilities. The Presbyterian's General Assembly noted this when it developed a *new* mandate for the corporate social investment element at the 1970 meeting. Secondly, it still affirms a split between investments and programs which will (a) make coordination of all church activities more difficult and (b) again make very difficult the development of a *raison d'être* in which all church activities cohere.

Model 4 exacerbates the problems discussed in Model 3 by removing social investment even further from the church. It does, however, enhance the possibility of more ecumenically coordinated investment policies. A group of churchmen (including distinguished black churchmen, Wall Street attorneys and businessmen), is currently developing a proposal which will cover several aspects of social investment through the medium of a mutual fund which is linked to a newly formed foundation. If accepted by the SEC, the mutual fund will be open to both institutions and individuals. A reputable investment group will manage the fund and will be guided, in turn, by a separate "social criteria" committee. This latter committee will evaluate corporate performance in specified areas and submit two lists to the fund managers. One will specify corporations in which the fund will not invest for social reasons; the other will specify corporations whose social performance is admirable and whose attractiveness as an investment opportunity on financial grounds should be carefully watched. The most innovative facet of this fund, however, is that the investor will have a specified upper limit of return from his funds. Any return over the limit will go into a foundation whose board will be made up of representatives of several national civil rights groups. The foundation will then distribute the assets gained from high investment yield in either grant or loan form.

At least two important elements of a total social investment policy are missing in this proposal: (1) no provision is made in the document being drawn at the time that this book was written for proxy voting or initiatives, and (2) the "creative" investment element is only derivatively provided for since the foundation would be using only investment income and not principal to support developing areas of the economy. Although it would be possible to build in a "proxy voting" or initiative element within the framework of the existing proposal, the "creative" investment element would not fit. Sponsors are convinced that strong investment counsel will enable the fund to do as well for church investors as they have done in recent years and still provide a sizable amount of "overflow for the foundation." [3] Persons related to the

[3] Information about this effort can be obtained by writing the National Council of Churches, 475 Riverside Drive, New York, N.Y. 10027.

United Methodist Church Board of Christian Social Concerns have initiated a similar fund, the Pax World Fund, concentrating investments specifically in corporations not involved in the production of armaments and with strong "fair employment practices" records.

Two words of caution about the possible proliferation of investment funds using social investment criteria are in order. In the next few years, as individual and institutional investors begin to develop (and begin to have trouble implementing) social investment policies, many groups can be expected to establish such funds. If the church investor takes seriously the discussion in chapter 2, he will want to make sure that his social investment policy and decisions do reflect his church's *raison d'être,* its own stated church policies and its own thinking on the substantive, contemporary ethical issues. Not just any— and in some cases none—of the "social criteria" developed by various external organizations will meet these requirements. While the church may not be able to be a "purist" on this matter and still do the job, thorough examination of newly offered funds that claim to do socially conscientious investing will surely be in order. The mutual funds promising to use social criteria will generally avoid corporations with bad practices and give special consideration to companies with good ones. It was argued in the first chapter that this option is the least effective, for, while it may help "cleanse" the church, it will do little about the deleterious practices of those corporations which it chooses to avoid. In addition, such funds probably will not utilize the "creative investment's options discussed earlier.[4]

THE INFORMATIONAL ELEMENT

It is truly astonishing that the social investment movement has gotten so far on so little "hard" information. Those who argue that the advocates of specific social investment initiatives have almost capriciously urged the church to pursue specific issues are not altogether wrong. As suggested earlier, the church will have to act without complete information for reasons of human finitude; finitude, however, is no excuse for being ill-informed. Two of the areas in the society's life where the least is known are the actual practices and workings of American corporations and the possibilities for aiding the economic development of

[4] An apology should be made at this point. This book has not directed attention to the special problems that independent theological seminaries (as distinguished from those whose finances are handled by a university) will have in developing social investment policies. On the one hand, a seminary is a "church"; on the other hand, it is an "educational institution." A church is free—indeed required —to live out its theological understanding in what it does. An educational institution, on the other hand, has special problems relating to "academic freedom" which will limit the scope of social investment initiatives. Some sort of amalgam of the suggestions made in this book and those made in the study of social investment policies of universities soon to be published is necessary. The seminary is more a church than a university, but the author has not yet developed his own understanding of what that means in specific terms. This represents an important caveat in the book since some of the first and most enthusiastic efforts in social investment have originated in and focused upon the seminaries.

those who have thus far been excluded from the nation's economic life. There is simply a crying need for information *and* for organizations to research and compile such information. What research has been done on the American corporation tends to be either totally sympathetic to or utterly dissatisfied with all corporate practice. Such research provides only a part of the information that the social investor will need to know. Efforts are now being made in several quarters to organize such research efforts. The Council on Economic Priorities, an organization whose founding was announced in April of 1970 and was widely publicized in the press, may be a prototype of such a research center. The Council will have published two books on corporate research by the time this book appears. One focuses on corporations involved in the production of anti-personnel weapons;[5] the other offers a more comprehensive study of seventy corporations. The Council also publishes the Economic Priorities Report and plans a number of further studies, including those which concentrate on the various aspects of the pollution problem, Southern Africa, and minority hiring in the hotel industry.[6] In addition to the Council, a variety of other fledgling efforts are researching corporate activities. Ralph Nader has developed a very sophisticated *consumer* research organization and has published several

[5] Council on Economic Priorities, *Efficiency in Death: The Manufacturers of Anti-Personnel Weapons* (New York, 1970).

[6] Information can be obtained from The Council on Economic Priorities, 1028 Connecticut Avenue, Washington, D.C. 20036.

studies in that area. His studies may be indirectly related to investor concerns.

It is too early to tell whether recent discussions in a number of nonprofit institutions (including foundations and churches) will result in strengthening existing research projects or in creating a new research organ for the social investor to which existing projects will be related. It should be obvious that what is required is not simply exposé work, but wide-ranging data which will provide the investor with information relevant to his own priorities, and allow him to make informed judgments in accord with the religious and social values shaping his social investing.

7

The Personal Investment Element

Although this book has focused on the large institutional investor and his many problems, the individual Christian investor and the church which has a small investment portfolio deserve a word of attention. Although no figures are available, cumulative investment holdings of individual Christian investors surely far exceed the total held by the churches corporately. Christians also sit on many other investment boards in addition to church ones. Obviously, if there is a *raison d'être* which should guide the total life of the church, including its investment of funds, this is no less true of the Christian individual. The relation of his faith to his society should optimally be no different from the relationship of his church's faith to its culture. Perhaps we are all tired of sermons condemning a Sunday-morning Christianity, but the lesson is still there to be learned, and one of the places that learning can be honed is in the area of investments.

But what can the "little man" do when the sermon is finished? There is some solace in being a little man. Being one among many, most of whom are larger and more powerful, one can easily point to the eternal "they" as the source of society's problems. It is well to remember, however, that the professor who wrote to the steel company president (see chapter 2) held only twenty-five shares of stock. Although most small investors will not be able to start a derivative suit—or even a proxy contest—most of the other options described in chapters 3 and 4 are open to him.

VOTING PROXIES

An individual investor cannot take off the months of May and June to travel the country in search of the annual meeting of the corporations whose stock he owns. On the other hand, he does receive a proxy and, as suggested, the voting of proxies is likely to become a much more important matter in the years ahead. Many investors routinely throw away their unmarked proxies. Others simply sign them and mail them back. The latter often vote blindly for management since, if management so specifies, it may vote the returned proxy in many cases. In most companies the individual shareholder still holds the balance of power. One does not know how many share holders in the 1969 General Motors contest took the time to examine their proxies and hence how many, aware of the choices open to them, voted for management on its merits. One does know, however, that the votes of about 93 percent of them (approximately 800,000) were registered for management on the two key issues raised by the Project for Corporate Responsibility. Many efforts have been made in the past to persuade the small stockholder to take his prerogatives seriously, and none of them have been successful. But with the present movement of many larger institutions towards the utilization of stockholder rights, the small investor may not be alone anymore. While stockholder democracy may not be an unqualified boon to those who favor greater corporate responsibility, it would be, as Justice Tamm has recently seemed to indicate, a start toward preventing American corporations from becoming "personal satrapies implementing the personal, political, or moral predilections of a few."

CORPORATE PERSUASION

Corporate management may give a letter from a well-informed stockholder greater weight than a similar one from an irate consumer or employee. "Well-informed" is the key word here. If the individual concerned about fair employment practices does not know what the record of his company on minority hiring has been in the past, he may be overly impressed with a public relations man's assurance that the corporation is actively involved in new efforts in this area or that the corporation has X percent of minority people on its payroll. If he does not know the policies of the unions with which the company bargains, he may be easily persuaded that labor, not management, is deterring efforts toward increased minority hiring. If he does not make clear that he is concerned with corporation training programs and efforts to move minority people into more skilled and higher paying jobs or into management positions, then he may come away with a false picture of the corporation's commitment in this area. Management will tend to notice, however, those stockholders whose communications to them express an understanding of the complexity of the issues but urge further and specific reform measures. Many such indications of concern will engender even more response. The solution to most social problems is expensive and difficult. The corporate executive may rethink his priorities, if he knows he cannot hide behind a facile appeal to his obligation to increase stockholder profits because the stockholder too is concerned about other problems and has some idea of what it takes to solve them.

SALE OR PURCHASE OF STOCK

Personal investors, like those institutional investors who have moved toward social investment policies, have tended to try to keep their personal investment portfolios untainted. As mutual funds which promise to use "social criteria" develop, this practice may increase. Like his institutional counterpart, the small investor will want to examine those social criteria with care. Is the mutual fund willing to vote proxies out of social concern? Is the "social conscience" of the fund manager funded in the same way as the investor's, or does investment in such a fund merely provide a way by which the small investor may painlessly and effortlessly salve his conscience? If it is the case that the buying and selling of stock does not greatly influence market prices, then a "silent" protest or commendation will be totally ineffective if the shareholder fails to tell the corporation manager why he decided to purchase or abstain from purchasing a particular stock. Even if he does explain his action, shareholder divestment may be ineffective. (see chapter 3).

CREATIVE INVESTMENT

Some of the creative investment opportunities now opening up will be unavailable to the small stockholder. Investment in the National Corporation Housing Partnerships, for example, will not be available to the man with a few hundred (or thousand) dollars to invest. The need is great for a mutual fund that will concentrate on doing with pooled funds of individual stockholders what the large institutions are beginning to do in this area. But MREIT, for example, is open to all. Further, anyone may open a savings account with a minority-owned bank or a bank whose loan policy to depressed areas is especially commendable. The small investor who moves into this area, however, will have to rearrange his priorities significantly. He may have to anticipate that his investment yield will be lower than it would otherwise be. Like the large investor, he will have to calculate whether his resources are better used by seeking the highest return which he then puts to socially beneficial use or by having his invested money "work for him" in those arenas of society about which he is concerned. (The stockholder needs to be aware of a tendency to rationalize in such calculations, however.)

The individual might have an impact in one other area. Most Americans contribute to a pension plan, and most have no legal right to determine how the pension board's trustees invest their funds. Yet, as we have seen, pension boards are becoming an increasingly important force in the economy and may have legal prerogatives to employ their investing power with an eye to social consequence. A strong indication from pensionaries that they believe their personal welfare is affected not only by the pension board's ability to increase their retirement benefits, but also by what happens to the society between the present period and their retirement age could influence the pension board trustee's understanding of his role.

CONCLUSION

In 1968 Jack Mendelsohn, a Unitarian minister, commenting on the social deployment of church funds, wrote: "There are no maps. On the question of investment policy, with its staggering stakes, there is no carefully worked-out rationale, let alone fiduciary law support, for novel social approaches." [1] At the time Mendelsohn wrote, there were very few indications that the churches would soon take an interest in the social consequences of their investment policies. Hence, he argued: "Church social investment policy is now more insulated from the com-

[1] *The Religious Situation: 1968,* ed. Donald Cutler (Boston, 1968).

prehensive concerns of human living than much of industry and commerce." [2]

While this statement is still accurate, it needs to be qualified in some instances. Many church boards across the country have been facing the social investment issue in the past two years; some have attempted to avert their eyes from it, but many have not. Still, since no "worked-out rationale" yet exists, most efforts have been *ad hoc* initiatives, longer on good intentions than on careful and informed thinking about where the churches are going and want to be going as they enter this new and difficult arena.

As was acknowledged in the preface, this book does not provide that rationale. It does, however, present many of the elements required for developing a comprehensive view. The author will have accomplished his intent if this book raises the level of the dialogue and spurs serious Christian reflection about what it means to be the investing church in contemporary America. Hopefully, this book has shown the reader that the rhetoric of both "There is nothing we can do" and its counterpart, "You could do it easily if you wanted to," is misplaced. The first is normally the rhetoric of those who stand behind legal doctrines which, upon further examination, are inadequate shields. It also assumes that it is impossible to change impeding law where legal problems arise. Every investor in the nation can do something.

But social investment is not easy. It is not always

[2] *Ibid.,* p. 957.

recalcitrance or sloth which makes men shy away from the suggestions made in this book. Men steeped and competent in a traditional way of doing things will, frankly, not find it easy to accept the new. On the other hand, those who advocate a change in investment policies will be more successful if they learn the complexities and the difficulties of what they propose and not slide over them into eloquent theological appeals which they cannot support with the legal, economic, and other data which will make their theology work.

Three questions are always involved in change. Where are we? Where do we want to go? and How do we get there? Not enough people know where we are! As suggested in chapter 2, not all Christians agree about where their faith requires them to go. Once this is clarified (and I *am* suggesting a chronology here), the hard work of figuring out how to get there begins. Developing social investment is one of the contexts the church can work in to carry out the tasks and arrive at the goals which its faith dictates. The imperative to develop significant social investment efforts in the churches involves these three components of change on a bewildering number and variety of levels. That is what makes it so difficult; but it is also part of what makes the challenge which this imperative presents so exciting and perhaps so exceedingly important for the church in the 1970's.

Appendix A: What Is Corporate Responsibility?

Not all perceptive observers of the American scene have universally hailed the shift in the language of corporate executives from unquestioned acceptance of the profit motive as the engine which has "made America great" to "corporate social responsibility" as the banner under which business will now help solve the nation's social crisis. Critics challenge talk about "corporate responsibility" on essentially two grounds: (1) that it is a smokescreen (albeit one with great public relations value) and reflects no important change in business practice at all, and (2) that if it ever should be more than rhetoric, it will be bad social policy.[1]

[1] Elaboration of these two points is imperative:

1. J.A.C. Hetherington suggests that management's acceptance of "responsibility" language has three primary motivations, all of which spring from its desire to retain its autonomous position of great power in the face of converging social pressures. According to Hetherington, such statements are intended to serve the following purposes: (a) they assert to the stockholders the right and duty of management not to devote its efforts solely to the stockholders' interest (and hence to pursue its own or the company's long-range interest at the cost of adequate dividends); (b) they suggest to employees, suppliers, dealers, and customers a benign concern for their welfare and thus implicitly reject the inevitable conflict between managerial goals and the interests of these groups; and (c) they suggest to the public at large that the businessman may legitimately hold and exercise the power at his disposal since he is a public servant who can be trusted to act in the public interest. (See "Fact and Legal Theory: Shareholders, Managers and Corporate Responsibility," *Stanford Law Review,* Vol. 21, January, 1969, pp. 247-48)

2. As early as 1958 and 1959, Theodore Leavitt and Eugene Rostow, now joined by Hetherington, Milton Friedman, and others, called upon business to eschew language and ventures which lead them away from primary if not single-minded concern for profit and economic growth. Four closely related arguments support their position: (a) it is only on the basis of their ability to turn a profit that businessmen can evaluate themselves and be evaluated by their peers, the stockholder, the government, and others; (b) the overlapping of the spheres of business and government which corporate acceptance of social welfare duties involves will hinder government regulation of business and will further erode the private-public distinction which these critics believe is still the means by which the twin objectives of economic strength and "life, liberty and the pursuit of happiness" are possible under the American Constitution; (c) that the businessman is without authority and an adequate perspective to adjudicate competently and equitably the competing claims of various interest groups; and (d) that with the bewildering complexity of social problems which distract them, the businessman will fail to carry out the functions in which he is competent, i.e., functions which provide the economic means enabling government and other groups in the society already organized to solve social ills to attack them.

Appendix A: What Is Corporate Responsibility?

One can only agree that "corporate responsibility" is an elusive and potentially self-serving concept and that it can obfuscate rather than clarify the way in which social problems can be solved. It can be argued, however, that the critics cited do not account adequately for the developments in American economic and political history outlined in chapter 1, and consequently ask business and government to turn the clock back to a period which it would be difficult, if not impossible, to recover. They may also not take seriously the "crisis of legitimacy," which has virtually forced the business community to adopt a new stance, and the growing body of businessmen who do not regard "social responsibility" as a dodge.[2]

Wherever churchmen stand on this question, it will be imperative, as they invest their own and the church's funds, that they understand (a) the various views of the corporation's nature and objectives which business executives es-

---

(See Theodore Leavitt, "The Dangers of Social Responsibility," *Harvard Business Review,* September-October, 1958, pp. 41-50; Eugene Rostow, "To Whom and For What Ends Are Corporate Managements Responsible," *The Corporation in Modern Society*; Hetherington, *Ibid.*; Milton Friedman, "The Social Responsibility of Business Is to Maximize Profits," *The New York Times Magazine,* September 13, 1970.)

[2] See Jules Cohn, "Is Business Meeting the Challenge of Urban Affairs?" *Harvard Business Review,* March-April, 1970. This important article is a product of interviews with executives from 247 major corporations, representatives of community groups, and government officials. This appendix has also been informed by responses to letters sent by the author to 50 presidents and board chairmen of the nation's largest industrial firms, banks, insurance companies and retailers. Essentially these letters asked executives how they understood corporate responsibility and what they were doing (and through what corporate structures they were seeking) to implement that understanding.

pouse and what they entail; (b) why they do or do not want corporations to undertake objectives other than profit maximization and growth; (c) what specific areas or aspects of corporate life concern them as churchmen, and how they want corporations to pursue objectives in those areas; and (d) how they think corporations can best organize themselves to carry out social goals. No social investment policy concerned with corporate practice will be meaningful or effective until these questions are directly addressed and answered. Consistent with all other parts of this book, this appendix does not propose the answers. It attempts only to break down the "elements" so that the questions may be seen clearly.

WHAT IS A CORPORATION'S PURPOSE?

At present, three definitions of corporate purpose appear to be operative: (1) that the primary objective of business is societal well-being; (2) that the primary (or only) objective of business is profit and economic growth; and (3) that business has several objectives, among them profit and societal good, which must somehow be kept in relation to each other.

1. B. R. Dorsey, President of Gulf Oil, has recently taken the first position: "Today maximum financial gain, the historic number-one objective, is forced into second place whenever it conflicts with the well-being of society. We must now examine the proposition that the first responsibility of business is to operate for the well-being of society." [3] This is an extraordinary statement. Immediately one wants to know

[3] "Business Responsibility to Society," Remarks to the Pittsburgh Chapter of the National Association of Accountants, 1970.

how Gulf Oil has reshaped its mode of operations, a reshaping which this shift in basic objectives should involve. He also wants to know who defines the "well-being of society." President Dorsey has given some answers. He accepts the principle of foreign operations in general managed by nationals; he gives business the primary responsibility for eliminating pollution; he also suggests that "our jury is the public."

Those who are now protesting Gulf's involvement in the Portuguese colonies (which, they contend, provides the racist governments throughout the areas with increased tax revenues and badly needed, indigenously produced petroleum reserves) will want to know how the jury is to be heard.

2. Roger Blough, former Chairman of the Board of the U.S. Steel Corporation, retains the traditional view of corporate purposes that profit and economic growth are the primary objectives of business.

It is true that the need for business to discharge a proper measure of social responsibility as a corollary need to that of operating profitably, is not always clear to us [businessmen] . . . . But what others frequently fail to comprehend is that a main ingredient for social progress is the increased wealth—the rise in the standard of living—which accrues to the country as a result of competitive initiative, technological innovation, and the investment and reinvestment of capital. Producing this main ingredient was and is the business of business, a function which it is uniquely capable of performing.[4]

[4] "An Address at the Annual Meeting," American Iron and Steel Institute, May, 1969.

It is true that Mr. Blough stresses increased hiring of minority peoples, better education and more adequate housing, but the primary goal, indeed the business of business, is business.

Closely related to this view and subsumable under this second category is that of Henry Ford II, who argues that the profit motive remains the goal of business but is more and more circumscribed by societal needs; indeed, social expectations become the only viable means through which to pursue profits! "From the standpoint of business, profit is the end and public service the means. Business earns profit by serving public needs—but profit and not service is the goal of business. From the standpoint of society and its members, on the other hand, service is the end and profit is the means." [5]

3. The third definition of corporate purpose, which suggests that business includes both profit and societal good among its objectives, is more subtle and allows for several ways of relating corporate goals.

a. One is taken by David Rockefeller, President of Chase Manhattan Bank:

Profit must remain the yardstick, because it is the measure of our efficiency, but profit must be based more and more on calculations of social costs and benefits as well as private costs and benefits. We must accept the fact that economic growth is not an end in itself, but rather a means to a greater number of social as well as private ends. [6]

[5] *The Human Environment and Business* (New York, 1970).
[6] Quoted in *Public Affairs,* Chase Manhattan Bank (New York, Vol. X, no. 1, 1970).

b. The other basic way of construing the profit-social bene-fit relationship is to see them as competing goals or pur-poses. Robert J. Weston, General Manager of the Building Products Division of Boise Cascade, feels that the business-man must pursue two goals. He must:

> . . . identify needs in the future marketplace that offer oppor-tunities for business profit and identify needs in the society that offer opportunities for service to society, then vigorously pursue both goals. . . . If we accept the validity of pluralistic goals for the American corporation, then the structure and performance of business will change right along with the change in business goals.[7]

All of the executives quoted above view the business man-ager as a man who must reconcile or choose between a plurality of competing interests (most of which are in some way legitimate). This schema shows, however, that corpor-ate managers differ over what their goals should be as they choose among the claims. Any investor who seriously wants to help the corporation be responsible will have to be aware of the nuances of these various positions on business goals and to clarify the relative merits of each.

WHY CORPORATE RESPONSIBILITY?

Closely related to the problem of corporate goals is the issue of *why* business now does or does not have social re-sponsibilities. Three basic rationales have been advanced:

[7] An address "Making a Place for Tomorrow's Managers," re-printed in *Business and Social Progress,* ed. Clarence C. Walton (New York, 1970), p. 26.

(1) that the corporation is more competent than other institutions to deal with social problems; (2) that it is in the corporation's interest to solve social ills; and (3) that the corporation has an obligation to pay the costs of its social effects on society. These are different, though not mutually exclusive, understandings.

1. *Because the Corporation Is Competent.* Corporation executives are well known for their scorn of governmental inefficiency.[8] Not surprisingly, then, they believe that they have the skills to solve the problems which the government has not yet solved in the present crisis:

> Many governmental leaders at all levels, federal, state and municipal, have increasingly recognized the limitations of public agencies in coping effectively with many of our social problems. . . . More and more business leaders are recognizing that the great technological and managerial resources of American corporations are critically needed in the tasks of eliminating poverty, rebuilding the cities, modernizing transportation, cleaning up the atmosphere and water, and bringing black and other disadvantaged groups into the mainstream of our economy and democracy.[9]

Businessmen differ, however, on the ways of freeing that competence to operate. Some see a closer and fuller coalition between business and government in these areas. Some ask government to clear out and simply to referee the corporate

[8] See Seymour E. Harris, Carl Kaysen, Francis S. Sutton and James Tobin, *The American Business Creed* (New York, 1962).
[9] William C. Stolk, former chairman of American Can, in *Business and Social Progress*, p. 66.

attack on social ills.[10] Others call for more government incentives in specific areas to provide the means by which business can attack the problems. Still others feel that because business is competent and government is indolent, business will have to go it alone.[11]

2. Because It Is in the Corporation's Interest. Other businessmen feel it is in the corporation's interest to become deeply involved. For some, using its competence for social betterment is a matter of survival; for others it is a matter of creating stable and dynamic communities in the long run (which will ultimately mean stronger corporate enterprise).[12] Insurance companies, which have the greatest stake in the economic long-term growth, have been the most active proponents of the view that their own interest is inextricably bound up with the health of the nation. Unfortunately, however, as is evident from the current recession, "responsibility" built upon these foundations is not terribly durable. Henry Ford, II, acknowledges this point:

> Now that public expectations are exploding in all directions, we can no longer regard profit and service as separate and competing goals, even in the short-run. The

[10] "I have often felt that while industry should be considered a player in the game of life, government must be considered a referee and rule-maker. As such it has no justification for also being the player." Henry G. Hohorst, *Business and Social Progress,* p. 45.

[11] It is noteworthy that fully one-half of the corporations actually involved in hiring and recruiting the hard-core unemployed are not on government program support. Jules Cohn, "Is Business Meeting the Challenge?" p. 76.

[12] "The principal reason industry is ready and eager to work on social problems is that these areas offer great opportunity for growth and profit, as well as for betterment of our society." Donald C. Burnham, President, Westinghouse Corporation, *Business and Social Progress,* p. 46.

company that sacrifices more and more short-run profit to keep up with constantly rising public expectations will soon find itself with no long run to worry about. On the other hand, the company that seeks to conserve its profit by minimizing its response to changing expectations will soon find itself in conflict with all the publics on which its profits depend.[13]

3. *Because the Corporation Must Pay the "Costs" of Its Operations.* One of the most interesting rationales for business responsibility, partly because it is both durable and potentially quantifiable, stresses that business must pay the social costs of its operations. There are two basic approaches here.

a. The more aggressive approach is proposed by William H. Dougherty, Jr., executive vice-president of the North Carolina National Bank Corporation. His is virtually the language of reparations: "It is axiomatic that private enterprise must answer the call because private enterprise started the whole mess in the first place. . . . Private enterprise, which started the whole tragic circle of events, failed to make even a token effort to meet these problems of the cities." [14] In a complex economic and political system the task involved in determining the actual causal connections between socially injurious business action or inaction and the resultant social decay is difficult, but some businessmen are now ready to undertake the task. Some initiatives in hiring the hard-core unemployed, especially those where government incentives don't make them profitable, are examples.

[13] *The Human Environment and Business,* p. 55.
[14] *Business and Social Progress,* pp. 51-52.

b. For others, "social cost" picks up from where things are now and makes sure that new and continuing corporate activities do not contribute to the development of any future deterioration of the social fabric. The recent statement by the board of directors of the National Association of Manufacturers, made up of 150 corporate heads, espoused this view and linked it with the competency argument.

The NAM acknowledges the obligation of the industrial community to participate in the solution of [social and economic] problems and to consider the impact of its own decisions and actions on the well-being of the total society. This obligation has particular force with respect to those social ills that are the direct or indirect consequences of industrial activity, or suggest action that business and industry have special competence to provide.[15]

Below the surface in most of these "reasons why" a corporation should take social factors into account is the acknowledgment that business is a "political institution" and must begin to act like one. One finds such a view expressed most clearly in a speech by Alfred C. Neale, President of the Council on Economic Development and former first vice-president of the Federal Reserve Bank of Boston:

We recognize further that the corporation is essentially a political institution, whatever its economic objectives may be. . . . A political institution must obtain the consent of the governed. The consents that are needed are diverse and vary from institution to institution. In the case of the corporations, the groups from which consents must be sought include managements, stockholders, the work force (with perhaps several different strata),

[15] From NAM's national urban policy statement, *Business and Society,* Vol. 2, No. 23, May 26, 1970.

customers, suppliers, bankers and financiers. Likewise included are the local communities, . . . as well as the various levels of government that are often customers, regulators and lawmakers —and in all instances, tax gatherers.[16]

Those churchmen and others who seek to alter business practices will want to know the reasons for their social involvement which specific corporate managements offer. They should be aware that the statements by corporate executives are not always lucid. They are often vague and seem to accept contradictory goals or premises.

CORPORATE RESPONSIBILITY IN SPECIFIC AREAS

Corporate responsibility has less to do with what business says than with what it does, however. The author's informal corporate survey concerning social responsibility revealed a most interesting trend: those corporations which provided the most impressive data on their actual involvement tended to be (or at least often were) those which had made less impressive public statements (and vice-versa).[17] Stockholders concerned with corporate responsibility will want, then, to test deed as well as word. To do so, they must be clear about which aspects of corporate life they will emphasize in their efforts to get "beyond the rhetoric." As a guide to this effort the following division of the corporate

[16] *Business and Social Progress,* p. 17.

[17] Jules Cohn argues a related point, that in 1970 the rhetoric of social responsibility dropped when programs to carry out that responsibility grew and when businessmen themselves discovered just how intractable contemporary social problems are. "Is Business Meeting the Challenge of Urban Affairs?" *Harvard Business Review,* May-June, 1970.

house may be instructive: (1) the corporation's internal practice; (2) its support of external groups and purposes; (3) its product; and (4) its influence on public policy.

Internal Corporate Practice

Much of the literature on business ethics focuses upon such issues as the role of honesty, fairness, integrity, and openness in the internal workings of a corporation. For example, "What do you put on the expense account?" Although these are not insignificant matters, they do focus only on issues of interpersonal morality and rarely relate directly to the larger internal institutional and structural issues which are this book's primary concerns. These issues include:

Employment Practices. Through such agencies as *Project Equality,* many of the nation's churches have indicated their concern for equal opportunity policies and have been a force, parallel to the government, in insisting upon corporate compliance. Equal employment, however, involves many things. In the present situation, the concern is not only for the percentage of minority persons employed, but also for corporate policies on recruitment, job-training, and the access of minority-group persons to the higher levels of the corporate structure. A corporation's success in one of these areas does not imply either success or strenuous efforts in one of the others. This fact makes difficult any evaluation of a corporation's responsibility in the area of employment practices on the basis of its participation in such programs as Plans for Progress, the National Association of Businessmen,

Project Equality and other similar programs. Much more precise indicators are needed.[18]

Labor Conditions. Unions are generally a more potent force for alleviating poor working conditions than the stockholder can ever be. Still, vigilance in this area is needed, especially where unions have failed to insist upon high safety standards (the mining industry may be an example) or where workers are not unionized. Again the issues are not simple. Involved are not only safety considerations, but efforts in job-enlargement (to relieve boredom from repetitive tasks), job-enrichment (including educational programs aimed at upward job-mobility retraining in the face of technological obsolescence, and increasing the estimate of one's personal worth), job security, retirement plans, and so forth. These issues are "old hat" in one sense, but for the persons involved they never are.

Plant Location. Government incentive programs will remain the primary factor persuading business to think in social as well as economic terms about where they locate their plants. Still, stockholder concern about this aspect of corporate practice could help increase management consciousness of the indirect effects of its decisions. A few corporations have even used the argument that it is necessary for their employees to have easy access to new plant locations as a way to break down restrictive or discriminatory zoning patterns.

Pollution. Initiatives on a broad front (including stockholder pressure) have resulted in more concerted effort in corporate research and development to reduce ecological and other effects of corporate production methods. (One rarely reads an annual report of an oil or other energy-producing

[18] *Ibid.*

company which does not include reference to these efforts.) Where government is caught between conflicting desires, on the one hand to increase revenues, and, on the other, to enforce stringent pollution legislation, stockholder concern about ecological matters could tip the balance. Since research data on the precise effects upon the life-cycle which different types of pollution cause has been slow in coming, *ad hoc* solutions have been the order of the day. Research breakthroughs in ecological research are occurring regularly, however, and an informed stockholder could raise the level of discussion.

Supply and Sales Practices. Although the number is small, some corporations have begun to seek out and support suppliers, dealers, and distributors whom the nation's marketplace has traditionally excluded. F. W. Woolworth, for example, recently announced a multi-phased program involving the Harlem community in its new two-million-dollar outlet there. The property on which the facility will be built has been sold to Harlem Freedom Associates, which will lease the property and convey the property to a local church which has appointed a "committee of representative citizens" to act as trustees for future income. A black contractor is building the store, and residents of the Harlem area will staff it.

International Operations. The character of international business operations has come under more intense scrutiny in recent years. In foreign countries there are often no "public" agencies with even the kind of countervailing power which the American public sector has, and growth in international trade will undoubtedly increase the potential for American dominance of foreign markets in the next decade. The proposition that business growth in developing nations is automatically a boon is as untenable an assertion as the one which claims that it is always a deleterious force. Increased stockholder monitoring of foreign hiring practices, wages, working conditions (indeed, all that has been discussed in this section) could serve an important purpose. Another serious issue is the extent to which foreign business operations shore up governments (through taxes and support of governmental programs) which have no legitimacy and would not have the people's support were it not for international business. On the one hand, one does not want American businessmen determining the public policy of foreign states and hence welcomes evidence that they attempt to remain a "neutral" force in the development process. On the other hand, "neutral" forces can often prop up socially reactionary and dictatorial governments. Informed and specific criticism or commendation of corporate foreign practices may be an increasingly important role for churches as stockholders.

Advertising. Government has brought corporate advertising under increasing scrutiny. The "truth in" legislation has greatly reduced fraudulent or misleading claims. But studies show that a variety of sales techniques and credit gimmicks still often exploit the poor. In addition, one can raise questions concerning the effect of advertising upon American life-styles in the light of evidence suggesting that advertisements can effectively create and change the wants and values of those who see or hear them.

Corporate Support of External Groups and Purposes. Businesses in a variety of ways may support projects and institutions which are not tied directly to the workings of the corporation. Corporate giving is a primary way, and we will look at it first. Of all the areas in which "social responsibility" involves a clear and nonrecoverable cost to the corporation, charitable giving has received the clearest legal authorization. The Internal Revenue Code permits tax-exempt deduction of up to five percent of pre-tax profits, and the legal precedents for allowing gifts only very indirectly related to specific business purposes are quite strong. Even so, corporations have stabilized their contributions in recent years at a small fraction of the allowable percentage: .68 of one percent[19] (although two large corporations regularly give the maximum allowable). It is noteworthy that the contribution percentage of the largest corporations generally is less than the .68 average. Some argue that corporate giving which is not directly beneficial to the company should not be dispersed by the management, but should be turned over to the stockholders to spend or contribute as they choose. (Proxy initiatives to enforce this view have regularly lost by wide margins.) Others argue that corporations are the one remaining major source of charitable giving with a growth potential in the country, and industry should be encouraged to increase the percentage given. While these issues are not insignificant, it may also be important for church investors to examine patterns of corporate giving and attempt to alter them if they feel the corporation supports inappropriate or ineffective charitable concerns. In general, education and civic organizations (the United Fund is a primary recipient) receive the greatest support. The National Indus-

[19] Figures from the 1968 triennial survey of company contributions by the National Industrial Conference Board (NICB). The Report may be obtained by writing NICB, Inc., 845 Third Ave., New York, N.Y. 10022.

trial Conference Board (NICB) estimates that no more than ten percent is earmarked for minority groups and urban problems. Still, corporations differ widely in their giving practices. Some oil and chemical companies (Shell Oil is an example) direct most of their support to the science and engineering departments in colleges and universities. On the other hand, one major industrial firm contributes primarily to black community organizations.

Skill-sharing is another arena of corporate aid to sectors of the society which have not fully shared in the nation's economic life. Many large corporations now free some of their technicians and executives from company responsibility on a periodic basis (a day, a month, or a year) to help minority-controlled businesses develop needed skills, write proposals, or draw up capitalization plans, for example.

Corporate Product. Distinct from both its internal and external management practice is the question of the social utility of the corporation's product. As we have seen, churches have traditionally not purchased stocks in corporations whose primary products were alcohol and tobacco. But there may well be a variety of other products or product features which a responsible investor will be concerned about.

a. *Product Safety.* In a highly technological society, one should be precise in making accusations that certain products are unsafe. Has the corporation failed to do adequate research? Is construction of the products poor or scanty? For example, some corporations in the drug industry are accused of marketing worthless and sometimes harmful drugs. As discussed earlier, anti-personnel weapons and other products for the military may well be considered "unsafe," to say the least.

b. *Product Effects.* Many products as well as production practices affect the environment. These range from pollutants emitted by automobiles to the present controversy over returnable vs. nonreturnable containers. In general, the products which America buys, uses, and disposes of, greatly condition its quality of life. As the economy becomes more service-oriented, the quality and purpose of the products it decides to make available become increasingly important concerns.

Corporate Influence on Public Policy

In a host of ways, what the government regulates or subsidizes is of paramount concern to the society's quality of life. As we have seen, the relationship between government and business is, today, not usually an antagonistic one. Hence, the church may have a responsibility to monitor what management tries to persuade government to do. Here are some examples. A church which views the establishment of free trade as a precondition to a healthy world economy may be at least as effective in expressing that view on a proxy statement or in a corporate board room as it is in church synod or assembly resolutions. A church concerned about environmental protection may find it important to persuade business not to attempt to block government proposals for pollution regulation. Extraordinary subsidy programs won through political persuasion can also affect the nation's priorities. Church and other stockholders should also be concerned that management does not exploit such subsidies or plumb for the "wrong" ones. (The oil depletion allowance or military-industrial relationships may be cases in point.) This is the most subtle, complex, and sensitive area of those which have been discussed;[20] it also may be the most important.

One should stress, however, that stockholder activities which pursue the alteration of corporate government relationships in the existing economic and political system are prerogatives of any part-owners of a corporation. The stockholder abdicates his responsibility when he fails to scrutinize carefully blatant abuses in this arena. It can hardly be construed to be an example of church "interference" in matters about which it has no mandate or concern.[21]

STRUCTURING CORPORATE RESPONSIBILITY

If corporate social responsibility is ever to be more than a public relations man's catch phrase, the modern corporation will have to find a place in its organizational charts for the men who will carry out that task. Changes in the goals and directions of large institutions rely heavily upon the structures which bear the weight of those changes. The organizational charts of, for example, the Ford Motor Company suggest the extent to which that company has recognized this fact.

And yet, executive Robert Weston's comment probably still stands,

I have yet to see an organizational chart that shows *how* the job gets done. . . . In truth it must be said that present organizational charts just have too many defects. They do not indicate the significance of the white space between boxes; they do not

[20] Part of the complexity is that business does not always use its influence in ways which the church will see as deleterious. Businessmen lobbies opposed to the war in Southeast Asia will be an example for those churches which oppose the war effort there.

[21] It is not, for example, an effort to determine public policy; it is an effort to keep *business* from attempting to determine public policy deleteriously.

delineate lateral communications; they establish artificial management levels. . . ."[22]

The recent study of urban affairs departments by Jules Cohn documents this observation.[23] Of the 247 corporations (from *Fortune*'s lists of the largest financial and industrial corporations in America) which Cohn studied, 201 now have some type of urban affairs program. This represents an important initiative by corporate enterprise, since only four of these departments existed in 1965, and most have been inaugurated since urban riots startled corporate management. But further reading of the Cohn article reveals the following problems:

1. Many of these programs are anomalous and have no abiding slot in the corporate framework: "We didn't know where to put it, so we formed a committee," one New York banker reported to the Cohn study.[24]

2. Few urban affairs departments have a clear line of access to the corporation's chief executive; many have been placed in personnel departments—which suggests a very limited range of activity; even more disappointing, forty are located in public relations departments.

3. Only seven of the urban affairs executives interviewed plan to make their careers in this arena of corporate life; many see their assignment as a "dead end" or wonder whether they have been shunted off to the side in the battle to the top.

4. Only five of these executives were trained in fields

[22] *Business and Social Progress*, p. 27.
[23] "Is Business Meeting the Challenge of Urban Affairs."
[24] *Ibid.*, p. 78.

which they felt were relevant to the new assignment. Most are trained in traditional business.

Urban affairs departments will need clear budgetary allotments and performance standards different from those operating in other parts of the corporation. And in order to be accepted as an important and permanent part of a corporation's life, they will need strong support from top management. Urban affairs departments in only five of the companies Cohn surveyed believed that they had such assurances.

A whole range of other proposals have been made for "structuring in" social responsibility concerns in a meaningful way. Some have proposed "public directors," including those who represent constituencies affected by the corporation (the Campaign GM proxy proposal included such a proposal). Others suggest (and again Campaign GM was an advocate) the establishment of a shareholder's committee with access to corporate information which would report to the stockholders on the successes and failures of management's initiatives toward more responsible practice. Others have suggested an urban affairs head, reporting to the corporation president, whose staff would fan out into the rest of the corporation and develop proposals for more coordinated social responsibility goals and efforts. A proposal not necessarily incompatible with those mentioned is that the "public business" of the corporation be given a "line" and not a "staff" function headed by an executive vice-president who also sits on the board and heads a "public business" committee on the board. By inventorying corporate resources and inventorying the problems which the corporation could affect, this "public business" department could develop more systematic approaches to social ills which the corporation could help alleviate and have clear access to the ultimate decision-making body to gain sanction for its proposals.

The notion that the corporation must alter its structure in assuming its new responsibilities is so new to most corporations that only massive efforts will be able to determine what is required. While stockholders may not be able to perform this task alone, it is appropriate that they spur the effort and sanction its results.

SUMMARY

Although corporate enterprise has become more and more concentrated in the hands of a relatively few managers, it does not follow that all corporations are the same. In one major urban area, one of the largest banks has developed a complex, wide-ranging urban affairs committee to oversee and develop more flexible mortgage policies, soft loans, and minority hiring programs, to aid marketing of minority-produced products, and to encourage bids from minority-owned suppliers and corporate giving. In the same city another large bank has adopted the rather strange view that because higher-risk loans might hurt the lendee in case of default, no such loans should be made.

The socially conscious investor has the task of discerning these differences and adding his voice to those who encourage the conscientious and chastise the sluggish. The potential of the American church to effect meaningful changes in providing for the health and welfare of this society may rest as much with the ability of churchmen to hone the powers of discerning the shadow from the substance of corporate initiatives in the area of social responsibility as in its efforts to deploy its own—and in comparison—scanty resources in the pursuit of those goals.

Appendix B: Church Documents on Social Investment

Included here are some of the most important documents in the area of church social investment activities.

THE UNITED PRESBYTERIAN CHURCH, U. S. A.

Investments in Housing and Business

The 180th General Assembly (1968) noted that:

The boards and agencies of the General Assembly be authorized and instructed that thirty percent of their funds invested, and available for investment, which are subject to no limitations on investment by the donor or by applicable statute or contractual provision be made available for investment in housing and business in low and middle income areas, some of which may offer a low return and a higher than normal risk. [This was designated Reference 5, 1968.]

. . . That the General Council be directed to report the nature and extent of such investments to the General Assembly annually. . . .

In order to clarify where final responsibility must rest when boards and agencies make investments "in housing and business in low and middle income areas," and in view of corporation laws, the General Council *recommends* to the General Assembly the following policy statement:

The 180th General Assembly (1968) at its meeting May 22, 1968, on the Report of the General Council under item U (*Minutes,* 1968, Part I, pp. 545 and 546), *inter alia,* authorized and instructed the Boards and Agencies of the General Assembly, including its Trustees, United Presbyterian Foundation, to invest thirty percent of their funds invested and available for investment, which are subject to no limitations on investment by the donor or by applicable statute or contractual provision in housing and businesses in low and middle-income areas, some of which may offer a low return and a higher than normal risk.

Some points have been raised by one or more of the Boards and Agencies and United Presbyterian Foundation as to their and their trustees' responsibility with respect to the authorization and instruction. They seek clarification on these points as follows:

First, the authorization and instruction concerns investments of a kind that are not subject to the ordinary rule of prudent investment by trustees, for it is stated that "some of which may offer a low return and a higher than normal risk." Hence, on the authorization of the General Assembly, there is no standard of judgment accorded to the Boards and Agencies and United Presbyterian Foundation in making such investments. Therefore, they, desiring to accomplish the intent of the General Assembly, ask that the General Assembly hold them harmless from any losses on investments that they or any of them state are made by the authorization and instruction of May 22, 1968.

Second, subsequent to the action of the 180th General Assembly taken on May 22, 1968, PEDCO, Inc., a Delaware nonprofit corporation, has been formed and is an agency referred to in item U, C, 3 of the action of the General Assembly of May 22, 1968. The Boards and Agencies and United Presbyterian Foundation request that the General Assembly confirm that investments made in or through PEDCO, Inc., whether by investments in it, loans to it, payments for loans made by it or participations in loans made by it, are proper investments of the kind authorized and instructed by the action of the General Assembly of May 22, 1968, and that the Boards and Agencies and United Presbyterian Foundation shall have no obligation to see to the adequacy of the investments or loans made by PEDCO, Inc., or the repayment of the same, and that a payment to PEDCO, Inc., by any Board or Agency or United Presbyterian Foundation shall be the sufficient acquittance of them and their respective trustees as an investment made according to the

action of the General Assembly May 22, 1968, without liability.[1]

Overture on Guidelines For Church Investment Policy—
from the Presbytery of San Francisco.

The 182nd General Assembly (1970) :

WHEREAS Jesus and the whole biblical teaching is consistent in calling upon believers to make their words and
deeds coincide; and

WHEREAS the Church has intensified its concern and sense
of responsibility for both peace, racial, economic and social justice; and

WHEREAS the environmental or ecological crisis imposes
upon the Church heavy responsibilities for witness and
mission with respect to man's stewardship of the resources
of God's whole created order; and

WHEREAS the Church's investment policies have for dec-
ades reflected its refusal to invest in tobacco or liquor
stocks, thereby indicating a partial recognition of the
Church's responsibility to apply ethical criteria to its investment program; and

WHEREAS the scope of the Church's vision as to the effect of investment on the faithfulness of its witness was

[1] Minutes, Executive Council. *The Minutes of the General Assembly*
of the United Presbyterian Church, U. S. A., Part I, Journal, 1969,
The Office of the General Assembly, Witherspoon Building, Philadelphia, p. 864-5.

recently broadened to include counsel against support of repressive regimes like those in Southern Africa; and

WHEREAS efforts to bring investment policy into line with the ethical and social teaching of the General Assembly and make investment decisions a conscious instrument of mission should be guided by a comprehensive policy rather than fragmented individual decisions,

NOW, THEREFORE, the Presbytery of San Francisco meeting in San Francisco on April 28, 1970, does hereby respectfully overture the 182nd General Assembly (1970) to direct the Council on Church & Society to:

1. conduct a study of the issues in applying ethical and social criteria to church investment policy, involving appropriate staff and Board members of General Assembly agencies as well as technical consultants,

2. prepare comprehensive guidelines by which the process of portfolio analysis and investment decision of all corporate entities related to the United Presbyterian Church in the U.S.A. (including, but not limited to the United Presbyterian Foundation, all Boards, agencies, and judicatories) can best express the whole Church's commitment to its mission in the world and its ethical teachings,

3. report the findings and recommendations growing out of its study and the suggested guidelines to the 183rd General Assembly (1971) and that, until such time as comprehensive guidelines for investment policy are adopted by the General Assembly, the 182nd General Assembly direct the Council on Church & Society to give counsel to United Presbyterian Boards, agencies and judicatories as they seek to bring their investment

portfolios to the support of corporations or governments that take the lead in reducing manufacture of, or dealing in weapons, in taking affirmative steps in overcoming racism, economic and social injustice and/or eliminating the pollution and exploitation of the environment.[2]

Action on GM Proxies Fight [3]

The Standing Committee on Church and Society began its work, to its own surprise, before it had had an opportunity to organize itself.

The Assembly moved with extraordinary alacrity to support measures that would provide spokesmen for the public interest within the structure of the General Motors Corporation. The action was taken just hours before the beginning of General Motors' annual meeting and directed that denominationally held proxies be used to support an enlargement of the corporation's board of directors and the establishment of a corporation committee to survey efforts to produce safer, nonpolluting automobiles.

Boards and agencies of the denomination hold approximately 113,892 shares of General Motors stock.

Early in the first afternoon session of the Assembly, Elder Harold R. Shannon stood to ask the Assembly to reorder its docket so that it could act quickly enough to be effective at the General Motors meeting.

He then introduced a motion of Presbyterian support for the movement generally associated with lawyer-consumer-

---

[2] The Minutes of the General Assembly of the United Presbyterian Church U.S.A., Part I, Journal, 1970, The Office of the General Assembly, Witherspoon Building, Philadelphia, p. 80.

[3] *Presbyterian Life,* June 15, 1970. Report on action taken at the 1970 General Assembly.

activist Ralph Nader. Shannon made his request in response to the pressures from youth delegates, which he deemed to be well-taken.

The Assembly referred Shannon's motion to the Standing Committee on Church and Society, which hastily convened in a vacant parlor of the hotel while many of the youth advisory delegates and other commissioners crowded into the room to listen and to speak. Most of the discussion was carried on by older commissioners, however, and almost all of it was vehemently in favor of the campaign proposals. The Church and Society Committee was unanimous in adopting a motion to direct that Presbyterian-held GM stock be voted for the reform measures. That evening, the Assembly concurred.

(Despite the pro-Nader action of several church groups and other institutions, only about two and one-half percent of GM stock was voted for the reform proposals at the GM meeting the next day.)

THE UNITED CHURCH OF CHRIST

Vote of the Seventh General Synod Establishing a Committee on Investment [4]

WHEREAS the Sixth General Synod

Declared that social values and social justice ought to be given consideration together with security and yield in the investment of funds held by religious organizations; and

[4] "Investing Church Funds for Maximum Social Impact: The Report on The Committee on Financial Investments," p. 53. This report can be obtained from the Office of the President of the United Church of Christ, 297 Park Avenue South, New York, N.Y.

Requested the Instrumentalities with substantial investments to continue to study the social aspects of policies and practices with respect to investments and to report on such studies to the Executive Council, and

In view of this commitment and the increased urgency to examine the financial involvement of the Church in the structures of American society,

THEREFORE the Seventh General Synod establishes a Committee on Financial Investments. This Committee shall be appointed by the President of the Church and shall be composed of seven members, one each recommended by the Board for Homeland Ministries, the Board for World Ministries, the Pension Boards, the Council for Christian Social Action, the Executive Council, the Council of Conference Executives, and the Ministers for Racial and Social Justice. The President of the Church shall be an ex-officio member without vote and convene the first meeting.

This Committee shall establish criteria and make recommendations toward substantial use of investments of all national Instrumentalities and Conferences to promote maximum social impact based on established General Synod policies. These criteria, upon the adoption by the Executive Council, shall be considered as guidelines for investment policy of national Instrumentalities and Conferences. The Committee is charged to report the results of its deliberations not later than March 1, 1970, to the Executive Council to be acted upon by the Council at its next meeting and to be reported thereafter to the Church at large. This Committee is to be funded out of the budget for special committees under the contingency fund.

After discussion and debate, it was:

69-GS-118 Voted: The General Synod adopts the foregoing resolution establishing a Committee on Financial Investments.

THE EPISCOPAL CHURCH

The Episcopal Church Ghetto Loan and Investment Program[5]

Black and other minority-group entrepreneurs, financed by loans made possible by the Episcopal Church, are beginning to make a go of it all across the country.

The Episcopal Church ghetto loan and investment program was established by the Executive Council of the Episcopal Church in the spring of 1968. It was set up on the recommendation of a planning committee of white and black persons, which included management consultants, corporate executives, attorneys, commercial and investment bankers, community organizers and staff of the Executive Council.

The objective of the program is to improve the economic well-being of minority persons and groups in both urban and rural areas in the United States through the development of successful minority-owned businesses.

The Church seeks to accomplish this objective by making loans to *"intermediary"* or *"umbrella"* organizations. These, in turn, either lend money to or invest in minority-owned businesses; they also provide management, financial, marketing, planning, and technical assistance.

The specific investment criteria used in selecting these intermediaries or "umbrella" organizations include:

1. *Indigenous leadership* must have an influential voice in the intermediary's program and in identifying and working

[5] These are excerpts from the November, 1969 report of this program.

directly with ghetto entrepreneurs to provide the necessary management advice and technical assistance.

2. *Profit-making enterprises* must be the ultimate recipients of the investment money. The objective is to build successful well-managed businesses. The borrower is expected to be able, in time, to repay loans.

3. *A "buy-back" clause,* whenever purchase of equity by the church is involved, is always provided to the enterprise. This enables the minority group entrepreneurs to buy out the equity interest held by either the intermediary financing organization or the Church, when desirable.

4. The committee is not interested in financing small "mom and pop" enterprises, since an important goal is the development of successful, well-managed, profitable businesses that will grow and provide good jobs, fine business training and equity participation for many.

5. The committee will not make direct loans to individual businesses because it does not have the staff or personnel necessary to supervise and manage such an operation, services better provided by intermediary organizations.

An important underlying purpose of this program is to stimulate more "umbrella type" organizations in communities throughout the United States. As previously indicated, these will, in turn, provide the vital ingredients of sound management and appropriate and adequate financing of minority-owned and controlled businesses to help make them successful and profitable.

An "umbrella" organization may be a profit or nonprofit corporation, organized by white or minority leaders, which can receive grants, raise equity or borrow funds and make these funds available to indigenous businesses being developed by minority enterpreneurs.

INDEX